Lost Civilizations: 10 Societies that Vanished Without a Trace

By Michael Rank

Table of Contents

Introduction

How Does a Civilization Disappear?

For a civilization that disappeared from earth over 1,000 years ago, the Mayas – better known as the Mayans – have had an extraordinary level of influence in the 21st century. On December 21, 2012, the world waited with baited breath at the conclusion of the 5,125-year "Long Count" Maya calendar, which many pseudo-intellectuals said was the official marking of the end of the world.

It is easy to laugh at such hysteria on this side of the event, but there were many who did not find the warning nearly so funny. The Telegraph wrote in the weeks preceding the ersatz apocalypse that the panicked buying of candles and essentials were reported across the world, from China to Russia. There was a massive uptick in sales of survival shelters in America from small manufacturers, jumping from an average of one purchase a month to one a day. Many French prepared to converge on a mountain where they believed aliens would rescue them. Turks gathered in the scenic town of Şirince, formerly a Greek wine production center, as the best location to weather out Judgment Day.

To cash in at the box office on the growing fear of Planet Earth's impending doom, director Roland Emmerich even saw fit to produce a piece of forgettable disaster porn staring John Cusack, appropriately named "2012." While it is doubtful that the film contributed much to the Judgment Day hysteria, it at least had an impact in China. The film was popular there due to its plot point of the Chinese military saving humanity by building massive arks. This is perhaps the largest irony of the Maya apocalyptic fever: it managed to impact an Asian nation of over 1 billion citizens, many of whom have no religious belief.

It is clear that nothing happened on that fateful December 21, but it is far less clear what actually happened to the Mayas many centuries ago. After all, how does a civilization that builds massive temples and famed cities-turned-tourist-sites, such as Chichen Itza, disappear quietly? It is a question that has baffled historians for nearly as long of a period, as their downfall was not a fast process nor were they wiped out in a day by a volcanic eruption or asteroid impact; rather, they seem to have dwindled and declined over the course of years until they simply vanished. What is known is that their disappearance came amid a number of large-scale migrations in Central America. In their post-classical period, the Mayas abandoned many of their cities in the southern portions of their empire, such as Palenque and Tikal, migrating north to settle Uxmal. This city was in turn abandoned, and Chitchen Itza was settled. The people of Mayapan, who in turn were conquered by Spanish conquistadores, ultimately conquered it.

The most common theories of the Maya downfall say that they disappeared from overpopulation or a lack of food. Perhaps the farmland was no longer as productive as it once had been, leading to famine conditions for the South American empire. Other acts of nature, such as epidemics, earthquakes, droughts, or fires, could have done them in. Warfare from neighboring tribes is another possible candidate.

Nevertheless, it is puzzling how a civilization that left behind such enormous ruins could disappear with nobody knowing the official reason. A lack of literacy in the society partially explains this phenomenon, since they left behind no written records, but their disappearance remains no less haunting to a modern person. If we were to observe an abandoned house with all its furnishings left intact, one could only assume the worst happened to its owners – whether it were a natural disaster, a brutal massacre, or an uncontrollable viral outbreak. It is for this reason that the mysterious disappearance of the Mayas, and the correspondingly strange apocalyptic warnings, have made legends and conspiracy theories surround their departure from earth. Did God eliminate them in one fell swoop? Were they abducted en-mass by aliens?

This book will explore 10 of the most famous real and

fictional civilizations that disappeared without a trace. It will explain the rise of these civilizations, the unique aspects of their thriving culture, and most importantly of all, the mysterious conditions in which they vanished. Scholars have offered theories as to how each of these civilizations ultimately disappeared, and we will look at the best explanations as to how an advanced civilization filled with bustling metropolises, vast trade networks, fleets of ships, and standing armies can disappear with nobody left behind to tell the tale.

Civilizations can die out in a number of ways. Sometimes they break down slowly over the course of centuries, as in the case of the Mayas. Other times, they disappear instantly, as in the case of Pompeii. The ancient Roman town was completely destroyed and buried under 20 feet of ash and pumice in the eruption of Mount Vesuvius in one fateful day in 79 A.D. With it were buried its population of 20,000, along with its amphitheater, gymnasium, water port, and complex water system. Its destruction is immortalized by Pliny the Younger's first-hand account of the volcano's eruption from his vantage point at the Bay of Naples due to his uncle Pliny the Elder dying while attempting to rescue stranded victims. Visitors can observe a city frozen in time and its citizens encased in stone like gargoyles surrounding the perimeter of a cathedral.

But most disappearances of civilizations are far more mysterious. This book will look at the civilizations that disappeared with no reasonable or clear explanation. Some are most likely fictional: Atlantis almost certainly never existed in the fashion described by Plato, since lost continents are hard to conceal, even if they are completely submerged in the ocean. If anything inspiring the legend did exist, it was likely a Mediterranean island that disappeared into the sea after an earthquake. Yet, the fact that the myth of Atlantis was so widely believed across the ancient world raises other questions as to what exactly the original lost civilization was that inspired it.

Other civilizations most definitely existed but leave us little clues as to the nature of their culture. The travelers that visited America before its European discovery left behind many curious artifacts, such as Roman-era coins or Persian pottery, but little explanation as to why they travelled to the New World and, more importantly, why they decided not to stay and colonize. Still others are well known to us due to the writings left behind by their members, but their disappearance is all the more cryptic as a result. The disappearance of the Roanoke colony in the 16th century at the dawn of the English occupation of the continent haunts us today, as the diaries left behind by its inhabitants left behind no clues as to the town's ultimate fate, other than a phantasmagoric message carved in the tree that read "Croatoan."

Civilizations disappear for a number of reasons, whether flood, fire, natural disaster, warfare, famine, disease, soil erosion, population resettlement, or any other number of explanations. Such disasters may have been so great that they compelled the inhabitants to abandon wondrous temples adorned with gold, or containing enormous pits of treasures, as in the case of Tutankhamen in 13th century B.C. Egypt, created in better times. Even if these cultures inhabit thriving agricultural centers, trade routes, or cities – their citizens may still leave at a moment's notice, shrouding their downfall all the more in mystery.

But rather than being forgotten in the dustbins of history as a failed society, the legends surrounding these lost civilizations grow. Ancient accounts of their disappearance in chronicles are based on the most spurious of evidence or distant rumors. The legends of these civilizations quickly transform into myths and take on a romantic character, all the more intriguing for people in the 21st century. Perhaps it is this mystique of the lost civilizations that convinced so many modern people that the Mayas, essentially an ornate stone-age society that did not even discover the wheel, had foreknowledge of an apocalyptic event that would destroy our advanced civilization.

The mystery of flourishing civilizations that were advanced for their time in history but suddenly ceased to exist and had all their temples, palaces, and houses abandoned make for plentiful conspiracy theories today. They also tap into a deep psychological fear that our civilization could suffer a similar fate. Living in an age of terrorism, nuclear weapons, and the potential death of millions if a weapon of mass destruction falls into the wrong hands has created much existential worry. After all, if it happened once in history with these lost civilizations, then it could very well happen again.

Let us now step back into history and explore the mysterious conditions in which some of the greatest civilizations in history vanished without a trace and hope that we do not suffer the same fate.

Chapter 1

Atlantis (9000 B.C.): Recovering Plato's Dream of the Fabled Lost City

Away from the hawkers of Cable Beach in the Bahamas, the lofty pyramids of Atlantis Resort glitter in the sun overlooking the soft sands of Paradise Island. There, tourists play in the aquamarine sea, lounge in pools, and swim with dolphins. The city is home to numerous international tax shelters, and as such, attracts the rich and powerful, who have the means to live in a state of luxury and comfort once only reserved for emperors and pharaohs.

What does not occur to the sunburned investment bankers who make up the resort's clientele – and the less fortunate resort staff consigned to serve them an endless number of Mai Tais – is that, according to ancient historians, poets, artists, and philosophers, just such a world once existed for all, and it did not require the cost of an airline ticket or the obligatory return to the drudgery of life on the mainland. An hour's flight northeast of Atlantis Resort, off the coast of Bimini, lies a sunken mystery that is one among many possible locations for what researchers hope to be the real lost world of Atlantis.

History's dustbin is full of civilizations lost to time, but in the case of Atlantis, the legend that was spawned by its description in Plato's Dialogues has only grown over the centuries and millennia. It has remained a mystery of enormous tantalization for thousands of years and has compelled researchers to spend millions of dollars to determine its exact location. Theories abound concerning the doomed society's final resting place, from the Atlantic ocean to sunken islands in the Mediterranean.

But did the greatest civilization that ever existed ever exist?

6

The only reference we have to the legendary island is in Plato's dialogues, Timaeus and Critias, written in 360 B.C., and it is not known whether the philosopher was writing history or fiction. Plato describes the island's destruction 9,000 years prior to his writing as a historical fact, but it is unclear if he is discussing what he believes to be true or if he is using the lost island as a heuristic device for one of his lessons. In antiquity, when Plato wrote his work, fact and myth were intermingled in daily life as a way of interpreting, predicting, and managing behavior. The gods walked the earth – metaphorically to some, literally to others. They were anthropomorphic representations of the elements. If the storms thundered about, then Zeus was angry. If the seas crushed a fleet of trireme vessels, then Poseidon needed to be appeased. A Greek farmer would discuss his crops in the same breath as beseeching Dionysus for a good grape harvest. Their deeds, and the deeds of heroes, served as a moral compass, a way to direct social behavior and define focus for personal goals.

In this context, it is easy to accept Plato's account of Atlantis as a morality tale, whether or not it has a basis in fact. Since the story recounts the victory of Athens over Atlantis in open war, he may be referring to Greek warfare with foreigners in times of ancient antiquity.

Whatever the nature of the story, later interpretations have gradually overshadowed the conceptualized ideals of Plato's fable with the possibility that his mythical island, with its shining city, was actually real. Although not a historian, Plato's renown as one of the triumvirate of ancient philosopher's titans – the other two being Socrates and Aristotle – lends his writing an air of authority that stretches beyond philosophy for many. Historians, pseudo-scientists, and theologians are quick to point out the plausibility that, while Plato may have derived his account from other myths, tracing the origins of myths far enough back in time often leads to a source of fact.

The legend of King Arthur and the 10th century Annales Cambriae chronicles; the vampire myth and the historical account of 14th century Wallachian Prince Vlad Dracula –

even myths of creation and universal floods that reach back to the earliest human experiences – all have some aspect of historical truth to them, which is what makes the legends so plausible. In the case of Atlantis, the legend is exceptionally captivating and enduring, thus making the attempt to separate truth from myth more difficult than any other legend.

Plato describes Atlantis in detail as a vast continent or collection of islands beyond the Straits of Gibraltar. It was a mountainous region with a long plain and a shining city in the center. Concentric rings of water and land, which also provided a bounty of naturally growing fruits, naturally protected the central island holding the city. The people reaped two harvests per year and lived in a virtual Garden of Eden, which was the size of Libya and Asia combined.

The kings of Atlantis were fair rulers who loved and nurtured their people, but over time, they became corrupt and power hungry, raising armies and invading the lands surrounding the Mediterranean. The inhabitants of the regions banded together to resist the Atlantean invasion, but all eventually fled under the insurmountable onslaught, with the exception of the Athenians. In the ensuing battle, the Greeks were miraculously victorious, but soon afterward, within a single day, Atlantis was destroyed by earthquakes and sank into the sea, leaving only an impassable muddy shoal that no ship could traverse.

Plato wrote that the Greek king Solon learned of the legend of Atlantis after a visit to Egypt, where priests related the tale. According to ancient sources, the philosopher Crantor claimed that Plato's account was corroborated by his own visit to Egypt, where he studied for 13 years under the Horite priest Sechnuphis. There, the history of Atlantis was found to be written on several pillars in hieroglyphics. These pillars have never been found.

Over time, the description, location, behavior, and technology of Atlantis and its inhabitants have been interpreted and exaggerated by a wide variety of authors, philosophers, poets, mystics, amateurs, hucksters, and other Atlantis enthusiasts. As time went on, Atlantis grew in stature, as did the Atlanteans themselves, who in some accounts became giants or demi-gods. While the priests and philosophers of antiquity treated the myth as nothing more than a fable and changed parts of the narrative to suit their own moral bent, later theorists concentrated more on the "real" Atlantis. The once mythical kingdom became the lost link to an idyllic utopian past; a treasure that, if finally discovered, might lead humans back to the beauty, creativity, and peace of a bygone golden age.

Is there even a kernel of truth in this myth? Could people have lived 9,000 years ago – thousands of years before the emergence of Egypt's Old Kingdom – in a city that rivaled Athens or Rome? From an archeological standpoint, it is difficult to believe. The most advanced city from the Neolithic era that has been found thus far is Çatalhöyük in modern-day Turkey. It dates to 7,500 B.C. and was a settlement of 10,000 people packed together in a beehive design, with little more to show for their society than pottery and arrowheads. If a city as ancient and advanced as Atlantis did exist, it would completely contradict 150 years of archeology.

But it is a hard fable to let go of when one hears Plato's description: Atlantis had ten kings, all sons of Poseidon, and the central king was Atlas. A separate military class acted as guardians of the land and dwelt in peace enjoying the same bounty as civilian citizens. The people shunned precious metals and sought to live not in excess, but with just enough luxury to make their dwellings aesthetic and comfortable. Before the fall, Platonic Atlantis was paradise.

The description has caused archeologists of other civilizations (of varying levels of credibility) to believe that it may have applied to societies other than Atlantis. One such group is the Mayanists, a diverse collection of 19th-century Mesoamerican archaeologists and romantics who were inspired to equate the mysterious disappearance of Maya civilization and its technological advances with the legend of Atlantis. Key Mayanists, including Augustus Le Plongeon and Brasseur de Bourbourg, suggested that the Mayas and Egyptians shared a historic lineage with Atlantis. Their temples, advanced agriculture, and seemingly idyllic way of life were exemplary of how the Atlanteans lived 11,000 years ago.

Others, such as the Theosophists, who were inspired by the works of Ignatius Donnelly and his thesis that all ancient civilizations were related to Atlantis, described the Atlantean way of life as almost otherworldly. The citizens possessed supernatural powers and psychic abilities, and lived in an Eden that was eventually destroyed by their own power. Helena Blavatsky, the co-founder of the Theosophical Society in the late 1800s, further modernized the myth by claiming that her own race, which she called "Aryan," had succeeded the Atlanteans as the superior race of the planet. Such mythical sentiments of racial superiority found dangerous expression in the Nazi Party in the 1930s.

Discussing the possible reasons for the disappearance of Atlantis has the potential to bring to light some of the actual facts that may have contributed to the legend. According to Plato, Atlantis disappeared without a trace: an earthquake swallowed the island in fire and destruction, and it was never seen again. Needless to say, this kind of disappearance makes a historical forensic investigation extremely difficult. But there are some theories.

A National Geographic expedition set out in 2011 to determine whether an area of marshland in southern Spain could be the location of the mythical Atlantis. The area was the former site of an ancient lake and contains remnants of ruins that appear to be Greek or Roman. The expedition theorized that a tsunami could have wiped out this ancient civilization, and they offered some evidence in proof. This weathered ruin, consisting of a few stones in the middle of an ancient lake, is a compelling, though meager, bit of evidence of a very early Mediterranean city.

Several researchers have suggested that Doggerland, an area between Denmark and England, could harbor the disappeared island. Doggerland is a shallow waterway that might be interpreted as an impassible "muddy shoal." Perhaps the most compelling piece of evidence is the geologic record of a tsunami or flood of glacial melt water approximately 6,000 years ago that devastated the area. Some of these facts fit well with Plato's brief description, but its location raises numerous doubts. Doggerland is in the North Sea, and while the location is indeed beyond the Straits of Gibraltar, it is quite a distance from Greece. Whether Plato or the Egyptians would have known of it is the subject of debate.

Bimini Road, an underwater rock formation near North Bimini island in the Bahamas, is another proposed site. Edgar Cayce, an early 20th Century mystic and follower of Helena Blavatsky's Theosophical Society, proposed it. In the 1930s, Cayce claimed that he had entered a trance and received visions of Atlantis as an advanced society with crystal-powered flying machines and electricity. As fanciful as Cayce's descriptions seemed, his prediction that parts of Atlantean temples would re-emerge "under the slime of ages and sea water near Bimini" in 1968 or 1969 actually turned out to corroborate with hard evidence. Strangely, just such a discovery was made off the island of Bimini at the time. The structures outline an ancient harbor, and several human-made artifacts have been found at the site in the early 21st century. However, there is no evidence of a people or infrastructure in the region that could have supported such an endeavor. Whether this is evidence of Atlantis or another as-yet-unknown ancient civilization is still the subject of contentious debate.

Yet another contender for the lost city is the volcanic island of Thera in the Mediterranean, which may well be the basis of the myth. A prosperous civilization lived there during the height of the Minoans, well before Plato's lifetime, and was wiped out by a catastrophic volcanic eruption. They were culturally distinct from the Greeks and had more power; thus their legend may have grown over the years to possess the mythical dimensions they held when Plato wrote down the specifics of their culture. Following its demise, Minoan civilization began to decline as well, concurrently with the rise of Greece. It is possible that knowledge of the island's destruction may have lived on in Greek folk culture and popular imagination.

The myth of Atlantis continues to endure in spite of all the debunking and the fact that most serious scholars and academicians consider Plato's account pure allegory. He was likely dealing with literary themes that frequently ran through his work: the divine versus human nature, ideal societies, and the corruption of human societies. Professor of classics James Romm says that the story of Atlantis is essentially an important morality tale of a spiritual people who lived in a highly advanced, utopian civilization. But over time, they became greedy, petty, and morally bankrupt. Therefore, the gods became angry because they had lost their way and turned to immorality. Such is Plato's intended lesson.

Yet, it is a dream that will not die. Many people in the modern era strive toward the ideal of Atlantis to harmonize technology with nature. It is also a good cautionary tale. Those who do not learn from the consequences of Atlantis's hubris, corruption, and greed are likely doomed to repeat its story.

Chapter 2

The Cucuteni-Trypillian Culture (4800-3000 B.C.):
Building a Better Society Through Creative Destruction

The Neolithic-age Cuceteni-Trypillian culture understood the idea well that in order to create, sometimes one must destroy. This was the way they treated their settlements, some of which contained more than 1,600 structures, and formed the continent's first great civilization. Each single-habitation site had a life of only 60-80 years before it was destroyed and rebuilt. Some were reconstructed several times on the same site, with up to as many as 13 habitation levels, leaving a deep record for archeologists to unearth. It is due to this policy of creative destruction that they have left behind so many thousands of settlements in modern-day Romania, Moldova, and Ukraine.

The mystery of their disappearance goes back 2,000 years to a period of Roman conflict with the "barbarians" of Eastern Europe. During the rule of Trajan (98-117 A.D.), Rome fought in the distant province of Dacia, an area north of Macedon and Greece, in order to put down uprisings on the Danubian Roman Province of Moesia and to acquire more resources for the empire. Following an important Roman military victory over the mighty Dacian army, a soldier climbed a mound of dirt to get a better view of his defeated foes' village. As he looked around his feet, he noticed pottery shards and strange totems that had been pushed to the surface due to the army's march to the top of the mound. Little did he know that these shards were relics left behind by a civilization that had flourished before the Dacians, and even the Romans. The soldier was oblivious to the fact that, long ago, this land had been home to the biggest city in the world.

Named after the regions in which the artifacts were found, the Cucuteni-Trypillian Culture was an advanced agricultural civilization in Eastern Europe that thrived for nearly two millennia, approximately 7,000 years ago. This Neolithic civilization built the largest cities in the world at the time, some known to have housed 15,000 inhabitants at a time when few other cultures were more than small collections of hunter-gatherers.

During each of its three major periods of development, the civilization grew in stature and sophistication, ultimately creating unique forms of pottery, tools, textiles, and farming techniques that pre-dated ancient Sumer. In the Carpathian Mountains of northeastern Romania, the culture took hold and ultimately expanded into the valleys and steppes of Moldova and Ukraine. At its height, the Cucuteni-Trypillian Culture consisted of more than 3,000 individual sites situated throughout the region.

As long ago as 4,800 B.C., the Cucuteni-Trypillians developed tools such as antler and bone plows, stone mill wheels, pottery, and weaved garments. They grew barley and wheat, as well as other grains such as peas and beans, maintained orchards of cherries and apricots, and are thought to have kept bees for pollination and honey. In perhaps the most important contribution to civilization of all, they may have produced the first wines (although evidence of wine production is currently still under investigation and has not been confirmed). They practiced both hunting and animal husbandry, raising cattle, sheep, goats, and pigs.

It was a culture of abundance. At the subsistence level, they were agriculturalists living in the warmest climatic period in Europe since the Ice Age and had access to a wealth of food and natural resources. This ease of access led to the development of a society mostly devoid of social stratification, since necessities did not need to be obtained from other more bountiful areas. Crops were grown on fertile land that was shared by all, and goods were produced and traded amicably depending on individual need. Families shared household chores and enjoyed a standard of living not normally associated with subsistence-level Neolithic cultures. The absence of large stockpiles of weapons indicates that this society was most likely peaceful, or at least capable of intimidating potential enemies into submission or pacifying them through trade.

Despite all of their social stability, the civilization embraced specific forms of disruption. Even the largest of the Cucuteni-Trypillian cities was not immune from the phenomenon of ritual destruction, a key characteristic of the culture. Approximately every 70 years, all of the villages within the culture were deliberately and systematically destroyed. Every structure was burned to the ground. Then the villages were rebuilt, most often in the exact same spot. Scholars argue as to the reason for this activity. It may relate to Cucuteni-Trypillian religious belief, which was likely centered on the fertility cycle of birth, death, and renewal. Their destruction of property, therefore, was done to appease certain gods and follow environmental rhythms of change and rebirth. Theories such as this abound, but to this day archeologists struggle to explain the reasoning behind this practice.

Another Cucuteni-Trypillian mystery involves the almost complete lack of evidence for burial or funerary rituals (with the exception of Late Period Ukraine settlements). The burial of the dead is one of the oldest characteristics of human civilization and its absence is strange, even in the Neolithic Age. Nevertheless, the bones of the dead are very rarely found at Cucuteni-Trypillian sites, and those that are found usually consist only of female skulls. The bodies are missing, as are any remnants of the men. This puzzling practice of decapitation may also hint toward the nature of Cucuteni-Trypillian religious beliefs, although whatever those beliefs might have been can only be explained by the morbid thought of what ceremonies that make use of decapitated bodies would have been like.

Among the largest number of artifacts found in Cucuteni-Trypillian sites are caches of totems and fetish statues - all of which are female. The presence of a large structure in the center of most Cucuteni-Trypillian villages, which has been found to house female figurines buried in the floor, has caused many scholars to theorize that the culture was a matriarchal one. These structures in the city centers are thought to have been places of worship and ritual activity. They may have also been used for fertility-cult practices, since the cosmology of many ancient societies mixed ideas of sex and reproduction with environmental phenomena like the weather, climate change, and natural disasters. If a drought was causing famine in the land, then a large-scale orgy could convince the gods to send rain.

Whatever the nature of their ideas about male and female roles in society, women were revered in Cucuteni-Trypillian culture, and fertility goddesses were worshiped through a variety of rituals. This might explain their practice of destroying and rebuilding an entire village as a kind of offering to the fertility goddess because it symbolizes renewal, but why and how the time periods for destruction were chosen is unclear.

One explanation of how their society developed to such a large extent was due to a very simple condiment that most take for granted today but was of enormous importance to the ancient world: salt. The Cucuteni-Trypillian was a salt culture, and its people inherited the oldest known salt works in Europe from an even older culture. The Cucuteni-Trypillians devised a shrewd method for extracting salt that involved boiling naturally salted water in ceramic urns and then drying it over heat to obtain crystallized salt. The spice was critically important for preserving food in an age that lacked refrigeration. This made salt a highly valuable article of trade, as it was scarce but of universal need, whether for food or in religious ceremonies and other areas of cultural significance.

The Cucuteni-Trypillian culture was also ahead of its time in the area of pottery, in which they achieved an unrivaled level of sophistication. Evidence indicates that Cucuteni-Trypillian potters invented a primitive potter's wheel, predating such a development in other parts of Europe by 1,000 years. Their pots were fired in climate-controlled kilns that featured two chambers separated by a gate. The designs were unique, decorated with creative shapes, indentations, swirls, and curlicues. The colors used were extracted from a wide variety of minerals, indicating a reasonable knowledge of plant dyes and extracts. Cucuteni-Trypillian log-and-clay houses often had two stories depending on family size, and walls were painted with the same swirling designs that adorned their pottery.

This civilization could also be considered the Neolithic capital of the fashion world – something of a stone-age Milan or Paris. Although intact textiles have not been found, most likely due their fragility and the environmental characteristics of the region, evidence of looms and knitting practices, as well as impressions found on ceramic items, indicate a significant industry around textile production. Despite the thought of clothing at this time in history being little more than rough animal skins, the people of this society were likely adorned in reasonably ornate dress.

The Cucuteni-Trypillians had many rudimentary devices at their disposal to build their structures and simple workshops. They constructed tools as well as weapons from bone, stone, and horn. They employed flint-edged scythes for reaping grain, and most likely used obsidian-tipped arrows and spears for hunting, judging from the absence of weapon caches and armories.

Despite being more advanced than their neighbors, they were not a self-contained society. Artifacts found in Cucuteni-Trypillian settlement sites that were foreign to the culture began to be seen during the culture's Late Period, indicating that a simple system of trade had begun. Stone and ceramic tokens found at Cucuteni-Trypillian sites are thought to have been used for bartering to represent certain goods like flour, wheat, or other raw materials. The Cucuteni-Trypillians would trade using these tokens rather than carrying their entire stock to trading centers throughout their loose-knit network of villages. Nevertheless, the reliance on foreign cultures for certain goods, chief among which was copper, may have signaled the beginning of the decline of the culture, which until the Late Period had relied on its own resources for survival.

After 1,800 years of relatively peaceful existence, the Cucuteni-Trypillian culture began to disappear. This decline was far from abrupt, spanning several hundred years and probably occurring settlement-by-settlement. Pockets of Cucuteni-Trypillian civilization lingered on into the early Bronze Age, but by around 2750 B.C. the culture was all but extinct. Researchers continue to debate what instigated this decline. Interaction with other cultures that were more warlike may have been a key factor. The Yamna Culture, which replaced Cucuteni-Trypillian, was a typical warlike early Bronze Age society. They brought with them a different administrative system and hierarchies of social status. The fertility goddess-worshiping, matriarchal Cucuteni-Trypillian people were likely easily overtaken by a society more adept at military conflict.

Yet there is little evidence of violent overthrow, and some researchers believe that the takeover was more cultural than military. As Yamna people traded and interacted with the Cucuteni-Trypillians, their more aggressive ideologies and strong social structure may have simply won out over time. A popular theory is that the Cucuteni-Trypillians were ill-equipped to deal with global changes in the late Bronze Age, in which increased trade and the growth of large empires required societies to have better security apparatus. The Yamna represented the invasion of several newer, more aggressive cultures that exterminated the old way of life across Bronze Age Europe.

As with many ancient cultures, changes in the environment cannot be overlooked as a significant contributor to the decline. A colder, drier period in Earth's history began to take hold in Europe around 3200 B.C. The incidence of drought increased as a long series of dry summers ensued. As primarily agricultural farmers, the Cucuteni-Trypillians would have been more vulnerable to environmental conditions than the Yamna, who relied almost exclusively on animal husbandry and hunting. Their advanced civilization was not as flexible as their nomadic brethren; they could not simply pack up their goods and move if the land did not yield enough produce. The dates of this climate alteration, however, are debated, and some sources indicate that they do not coincide with the period of Cucuteni-Trypillian decline.

The loss of the Cucuteni-Trypillian culture to many represents a loss of innocence, a fall from grace that has allegorical associations with the Garden of Eden. Characteristics of this culture were unique among Neolithic settlements, and with its disappearance went the religious practices, knowledge, and understanding of a way of life that was never seen again.

Interestingly enough, the Cucuteni-Trypillian culture was heavily appropriated by feminists such as Gloria Steinem and Riane Eisler in the 1970s. Many believe it was an example of an early stage of human development in which societies were run by women and free of all forms of war, division, conflict, greed, and competition. It was a golden age before the onset of patriarchy and all the world worshipped the Goddess – an idea echoed in such recent books as "The Da Vinci Code". The belief in a matriarchal prehistory, however, has been almost completely debunked in recent years. Philosophy professor Cynthia Eller argues in "The Myth of Matriarchal Prehistory" that such a theory is an "ennobling lie". In such societies as the Cucuteni-Trypillian culture, the sacred status of goddesses did not automatically increase female social status. Rather, it was the culture anthropomorphizing natural elements as being feminine or female, the way that the ancient Greeks embodied the concept of love in the goddess Aphrodite. Such ideas of a matriarchal prehistory, Eller argues, are modern-day projections onto the past rather than a historical theory based on solid evidence.

If anything lives on in their legacy that is based on fact, we can say it is a culture that was willing to destroy something in order to create something new. It could not have been easy for an ancient people to burn down their houses once every few generations, when the rain and cold threatened them with illness or death. Yet it provided them with a creative spirit that is in a way mirrored in the advanced free market economies of the 21st century, in which businesses rise, flourish, fall, and are picked apart – all in a matter of a few short years. It is this flexible dynamic spirit that allows old assumptions to be challenged, new ideas to flourish, and Motorola brick phones to be replaced by an iPhone 5.

For providing civilization with a template for this ingenuitive spirit, all iconoclasts and paradigm shapers should tip their hat to the Cucuteni-Trypillian culture, even if the ancient society itself was ultimately susceptible to this pattern of creative destruction.

Chapter 3

The Indus Valley Civilization (3300-1300 B.C.):
A Civil Engineer's Dream, Lost to the Ages

In 1856, General Alexander Cunningham, army engineer and archaeologist for the East Indian Railway Company, directed his engineers to lay track through the Punjab in order to connect Karachi to Lahore. They remarked on their good fortune at finding some old brick buildings in the area and reduced them to rubble for use as ballast for the railway. Amid that rubble, General Alexander uncovered a seal that looked to be written in the ancient Brahmi script.

However, research showed that it wasn't Brahmi at all; rather, it was a type of writing no one had ever seen. Cunningham was puzzled and sent it in to specialists for further inspection. They soon determined that those old brick buildings belonged to a city forgotten by time in an ancient civilization that existed long before England was even a concept.

The Indus Valley Civilization occupies a unique place in the pantheon of forgotten cultures. The largest and most complex ancient civilizations are known primarily because of the records they left behind in spite of the ravages of time, barbarism, disease, or invasion. Yet there are other, lesser-known but equally impressive societies whose characteristics have yet to be fully uncovered or understood. Chief among these is the vast Indus Valley Civilization (IVC), whose technologically advanced Bronze Age cities once ranged from northern India and Pakistan to Iran, surrounding the river systems that fed the fertile Indus Valley.

The IVC flourished for more than 2,000 years between 3300 and 1300 B.C., existing peacefully with other cultures of the same era. They engaged in trade; produced marvels of

21

art, architecture, and engineering; and supported a population of over 5 million citizens – 10% of the ancient world. It was geographically the largest of the ancient world's civilizations, as extensive as Mesopotamia and Egypt combined, and stretching thousands of miles from coastal areas in the south to deserts and mountains to the west and north.

Despite its large size and numerous extant artifacts, many mysteries still surround the IVC today, from their system of government and their religious practices, down to the name which they called themselves. Out of convenience, they are referred to by archeologists as the IVC or the Harrappan Civilization (named after Harrappa, the first city to be excavated in 1920s India) because nobody has been able to decipher their system of writing or discover their appellation. Other questions include the reasons for the ancient cities of Harrappa, Mohenjo-Daro, and dozens of others to be abandoned and the auspicious origins of the IVC's tradition of art, infrastructure, and trade. The biggest enigma is their high level of development. The society had a level of technology centuries – and possibly millennia – more advanced than any of their neighbors. What caused it, and, more importantly, what could have brought about their downfall?

Their end is mysterious, but their beginning is easier to determine thanks to the extensive archeological record left behind. Harrappa is one of the world's most ancient cities, probably having begun as a small village around the third millennium B.C. Blessed with residing at the cross-roads of ancient civilization, Harrappa and a network of villages began to thrive around the rivers of the Indus Valley. It and other major centers such as Mohenjo-Daro developed into major urban areas by around 2600 B.C.

Harrappa is an island of city planning, straight roads, and public sanitation in an ocean of thatch-roofed houses, rampant disease, famine, and primitive architecture that defined the Neolithic and Bronze Age world. It represents the classic urban layout of IVC cities: clean, well-planned communities that featured advanced conveniences like indoor plumbing, multi-story buildings, and private wells. These civil engineering works would not become standard features of any urban centers until the 19th century. Wide streets allowed for ease of movement and city management.

While Westerners consider modern-day India to be plagued by decrepit trains, vermin overpopulation, and pollution levels that would make jellyfish want to sign a Greenpeace petition, it was the Indus Valley that was the global leader in public health in ancient history. This was at a time when most European and North American tribes had barely figured out how to husband animals or bring in a successful harvest. The urban uniformity of IVC cities not only indicates broad knowledge of urban planning, but a population whose members all enjoyed a similar level of economic stability. There is little evidence of major differences in the social status among the population, much less the existence of a royal or ruling class. It seems that the Indus people either enjoyed a large degree of meritocracy, or the rulers did not see fit to live in a palace all that different from a common citizen's home.

This might be explained by theories about their system of government. One way in which the IVC people may have anticipated the Greeks is through their apparent egalitarianism. No one knows for certain, but the fact that no ruling class has yet been uncovered may indicate that the Indus people in fact had no rulers. While it is highly unlikely that a civilization with millions of subjects could govern itself in a utopian anarchy – after all, if unmediated forums such as Facebook can erupt so easily into petty squabbles among adults that resemble that of first-graders fighting over a pack of Lunchables, imagine such a phenomenon at a civilization-wide scale – most scholars assume that each city had a governor and that the state ran in a decentralized fashion.

The Indus people lived mostly free of disease and plague due to their highly sanitary nature. Most houses were outfitted with advanced drainage systems that led to central sewers. Each household had a flushing toilet and a means of rinsing waste away toward a central drain. Cities had hundreds of public wells where fresh water could be obtained, and many houses also had private wells. Cleanliness was supported by means of IVC engineers building large reservoirs and central baths. Possibly the best preserved bath is the Great Bath in the city of Mohenjo-Daro, which measures 38.7 by 22.9 feet (11.88 by 7.01 m). It is thought that the Great Bath may have been used for ritual purposes, but its true function is still not fully understood.

Their level of technological achievement in such a remote period of ancient history is baffling to modern-day researchers. Over the course of 1,000 years, the Indus people developed trade routes, built sophisticated docks along the river deltas facing the Indian Ocean that carried trade goods as far as Mesopotamia, and farmed the fertile valleys of their home. They grew barley; raised and husbanded animals, including water buffalo; and smelted copper, bronze, tin, and lead. Not only did they use these minerals to create tools and sophisticated architectural structures, but they created handicrafts and works of art that even today stand out for their ingenuity and creativity.

Although most of our knowledge about the IVC has come from the cities of Harrappa and Mohenjo-Daro, its origins may lie in the ancient city of Merhgarh, discovered by archaeologists much later in the Indus Valley region of Pakistan. Merhgarh was occupied during several major periods from the Neolithic to the height of IVC development around 2500 to 2000 B.C. Archaeological evidence from Merhgarh points to the development of metallurgy, art, agriculture, and even dentistry – although unfortunately for the IVC residents with tooth decay, there was no sign of ancient Novocaine.

Architecture aside, innovative engineering, art, music, and education also proliferated in society. Advanced mathematics contributed to a standardized system of weights and measures that anticipated the globally standardized systems of measurement (sans the United States and our beloved miles and pounds). Some theorize that Indian mathematics, many of whose principles still hold sway in the modern world, has its origins in the practical mathematics of the IVC.

Their ability to construct projects on such a wide scale comes from a tool as modest as it was important: the ruler. Buildings were constructed of bricks made using standardized measurements by means of a ten-point ruler, resulting in a uniform design that allowed urban centers to flow freely between wide streets.

The Indus people carved intricate works of art from lapis lazuli, ivory, and terra cotta, and even introduced personal hygiene products such as combs and makeup kits. The quality and erudition of their sculptures have earned comparisons to works of classic Greece, due to the works of art indicating well-developed systems of abstract thought and considerable creativity.

Religion in this society was as equally eclectic as its other characteristics. There is little evidence of a priestly class, although there are some indications that the IVC people followed a certain prototypical type of Hinduism with a loose pantheon of gods that oversaw specific human affairs and took on anthropomorphic or animal forms. Their seals, which are also the basis of their writing, depict animals and horned figures seated in the lotus position along with other figurines that might represent the goddess of fertility and other early Hindu deities. Still, the IVC cities had no temples or ritual areas, or at least none that have been recognized as such.

Lest we deify the IVC, it should be noted that the society was not advanced in all areas of development. For all their innovation, the IVC people never developed a system of irrigation for their crops, limiting the amount of annual agricultural output. This might not be a valid criticism, however, since they may not have found it necessary to do so. Heavy monsoons regularly replenished the soil with rich silt, and the seasonal rivers flowed with such regularity that IVC cities were often surrounded by high walls to protect them from flooding. Huge agricultural surpluses from regular monsoons were a cornerstone of their trade network.

For all its technological advancement, the IVC suffered the same fate as all other ancient civilizations. Due to the precipitous downturn in archeological remains after a few decades in history, its disappearance is thought to have been abrupt and sudden. After 1800 B.C., the IVC fell into a steep and irreversible decline. Whole cities were abandoned within a century. Trade networks dissolved. Production centers were either taken over by other civilizations or deserted completely.

In previous decades, a popular theory among archeologists held that the nomadic Aryan peoples from South Asia forcibly invaded but were unable to maintain the same level of urban and social sophistication. This hypothesis was abandoned when no evidence of violent conflict appeared. Others have theorized that it was the fault of an invasion of a nomadic and less-developed culture that led to the civilization's disappearance. It is a plausible theory with plenty of precedence in history. The fall of the Western Roman Empire in the fourth and fifth centuries was exacerbated by just such an influx of nomadic peoples such as the Goths and Huns pouring across the borders and sacking cities. However, archaeological evidence of a migration is meager, and most scholars have also discounted this theory.

Tectonic activity in the area suggests that the course of major rivers may have been diverted, leading to massive droughts and famine due to IVC's lack of a proper irrigation infrastructure. This theory is still being investigated, however, and scientists have been unable to match the timelines of cities whose origins have yet to be dated with evidence of geologic upheaval.

Nevertheless, drought seems to have certainly been a contributor to the civilization's decline. The Indus Valley was fed by a number of seasonal rivers such as the Ghaggar and the Hakra. During the monsoon season, these rivers would replenish the land, and during the dry season they would disappear. But from 2500-1900 B.C., many of these seasonal rivers dried up permanently. The tectonic theory purports that some of the rivers changed course due to land upheavals and joined other rivers to the east and west as tributaries, leaving the cities that formerly adjoined rivers to their fates. Today, many of the sites of ancient IVC cities lie along dry river beds, giving strong plausibility to this theory.

But what about the coastal outposts, and the cities that lay along rivers that continued to flow? They did not receive the same geographical death sentence as their sister cities, so what reason would they have had to disappear? After all, Harrappa itself faced the Indus River – Pakistan's longest river – which is still fed by waters from the Tibetan Plateau. One possible answer is that so many cities were devastated by drought that the consensus among the remaining IVC settlements was to move to more fertile lands to avoid the same fate.

Climate change seems to have also been a contributor, as recent geological studies have determined that the seasonal monsoon gradually moved eastward out of the Indus Valley and toward central India. Since the IVC people relied on monsoons rather than irrigation, disappearance of the monsoon would have been an insurmountable challenge. This change in climatic conditions, combined with a possible tectonic disturbance and the disappearance of two major rivers, may have signaled the death knell for the IVC.

What if the population wasn't wiped out or killed off, but simply decided to relocate? One theory of the IVC's decline is the Detroit model: a once-thriving center is abandoned over the years due to economic reasons, and its downward spiral accelerates as security decreases and criminal elements move into town. Whatever the reason for its decline, the people appeared to have moved eastward – whether to follow the monsoon, find more fertile river land, or escape hordes of invaders. Smaller cities showing the influence of the IVC were established in the Ganges basin, indicating that the Indus people may have followed the gradual movement of the monsoon. These smaller villages were more dependent on local rains and would not have been able to sustain the giant surpluses of agriculture enjoyed by Harrappa. Trade most likely dried up, and with it went most of the earmarks of IVC civilization.

Was the decline as abrupt as most scholars theorize? Perhaps not. To find out, we can look at the accounts of Alexander the Great and if he found any remnants of the IVC in his military expedition across Asia. When the Macedonian conqueror reached what is modern day Pakistan around 325 B.C., the ancient city of Pirak was among his conquests. This city was an IVC settlement continuously populated until at least 800 B.C. and intermittently afterward, gifted with the same agricultural and engineering innovations that were so prevalent at the height of the Harrappan civilization over 500 years earlier. Cities like Pirak may have continued to hold influence and given rise to the lasting legacy of India itself. In this way, the Indus Valley Civilization may have never quite disappeared, but was simply absorbed into daughter states.

In an interesting twist on the story of lost civilizations and the IVC, the people of the Indus Valley may have themselves contemplated the disappearance of another lost civilization at a nearby territory. Researchers in 2002 discovered underwater debris from a site at India's Gulf of Cambay that may be as old as 9,000 years – five millennia older than the Harappan civilization and dozens of centuries older than what are thought to be history's most ancient settlements. This find has already had massive repercussions on the traditional view of the ancient world.

Thus it is fitting that the Indus Valley people have left behind a lost civilization that leaves today's researchers puzzled. The ancient Indian society likely spent similar intellectual energy wondering about their forefathers and ancestors who left to them abandoned cities. Their similarly abandoned artifacts is perhaps the IVC's way of paying it forward.

Chapter 4

The Pyramid Builders (2700-1700 B.C.):
Skilled Craftsmen to Some, Visitors from Another Planet to Others

The year is 1990 and tourists are flocking to Giza. They brave the hot sun and threat of sunburn for glimpses of the timeless majesty of the monuments along the west bank of the Nile River. One such tourist takes to the sand on horseback, only to stumble over a crumbling wall long ignored by locals. He informs the authorities, but they are baffled by the discovery. They then phone in archeologists at a nearby research institute. Soon an excavation begins, and the researchers clear away a millennia of sand and dust. Their tools hit something solid. They remove the debris around the object; gold reflects back in their faces.

It is a tomb, and it is not alone. As the excavation continues, a vast cemetery forms around this lone tomb, sprawling along the foot of the pyramids. These graves, complete with containers of bread and beer to accompany their occupants into the afterlife, at first appear to be the resting places of royal officials. Further inspection shows that they are people that nobody expected to find buried in such ornate tombs: the simple workers responsible for the construction of the pyramids.

The enigmatic nature of the burial for these otherwise poor laborers is one of many reasons that these builders are a source of considerable speculation today. We have almost no information about them, except that they accomplished feats of engineering considered beyond the abilities of technology in the ancient world. The Giza Pyramids were the largest buildings on earth until the 19th century. The Great Pyramid stands at 481 feet (147 meters) above the plateau and is made up of 2.3 million stone blocks, each one weighing from 2.5 to 15 tons, yet they fit together as well as a jigsaw puzzle. The pulley system required to position such heavy stones so perfectly would have to be mind-bogglingly complex – that is, if they had access to pulleys at all, which they did not. In order to build such a massive structure without the benefit of even primitive technology, images come to mind of slaves being crushed under the weight of the massive stones or working in tandem like drones that are carrying a leaf back to the ant colony.

Other puzzling characteristics of the pyramids include the means by which the materials were transported to the remote site and the advanced scientific knowledge embedded in its construction. The stones came from quarries hundreds of miles away from the site and appear to have been transported in one unit. Furthermore, the Giza Pyramid complex lies at the intersection of earth's longest lines of latitude and longitude. This geographical knowledge of the earth's spherical shape and its exact dimensions remained unknown long after the decline of Egypt's Old Kingdom. As a result, many conspiracy theorists have speculated that the original architects were alien visitors to Earth who decided to lend a hand to the struggling slave laborers. Other theorists claim that the pyramids were built by a lost civilization – perhaps even the Atlanteans – whose advanced technology is no longer with us.

A step into history may help solve this mystery. The Greek historian Herodotus described the pyramids of Egypt in the fifth century B.C., noting that the monumental undertaking of their construction required 100,000 slaves working in shifts, toiling under the watchful eye of slave masters. Of course, Herodotus had not actually witnessed this phenomenon – the pyramids were already ancient by the time he began writing. Recent discoveries associated with the ancient tombs of the laborers also show that not only was Herodotus' estimate too great by about two-thirds, but the workforce was made up of honored and skilled tradesmen who were paid for their back-breaking work, not slaves.

The use of skilled workers on the pyramid contradicts common knowledge about labor in ancient Egypt. The image of a slave-driver with whip in hand, shouting orders at miserable workers to move faster or risk death comes to mind, but new evidence shows that it is based more on conjecture of the brutal nature of ancient societies than historical reality. New evidence not only shows that the long-accepted estimates of manpower and scale were incorrect, but it sheds new light on Egyptian society as a whole. Entire cities were built to house seasonal workers, and a scalable infrastructure grew up around them to support the ongoing effort. Pyramid construction was an industry in and of itself because of the longevity of each project, and required the mobilization of considerable resources. This meant that the ancient Egyptians had to be capable of organizing a massive labor force, design and build cities, and juggle astronomical costs.

Just as there were divisions of temple workers who specialized in duties associated with the temples, evidence of graffiti in the sprawling pyramid townships indicates that there were similar divisions for pyramid builders. For Egyptian laborers, the work may have been exhausting, but it was good work if you could get it. Pyramid builders lived in cities that benefited from Egypt's growing economy of scale and enjoyed all the luxuries of urban society.

They were served prime beef, goat, beer, and bread. They were commoners, but were treated as a special class, given tax breaks, and interred in tombs that were monuments to their efforts in building the final resting places of their god-kings. Other bits of evidence that indicate their room-and-board plan wasn't so bad include vast grain silos, evidence of cattle being imported from the Egyptian hinterlands, processing rooms for fish preparation, and bakeries dedicated to baking bread for large numbers of people that were discovered on the Giza plateau toward the end of the 20th century.

All of this evidence still does not explain how they actually built the massive structures. The sheer size of the pyramids at Giza is still overwhelming. These giants still dwarf the encroaching city of Cairo, lying along the Nile's west bank in the direction of the setting sun – the same direction as the Egyptian underworld. Seeing the pyramids provokes wonder in the viewer and puts a home gardening project that took weeks of preparation into proper perspective. Their imposing size and thought-provoking shape leads to astonishment regarding their construction. How could such marvels have been built with stone and copper tools but without wheels, winches, or pulleys?

Research has shown that construction of the pyramids, while certainly one of the most monumental undertakings in human history, was not something that could only have been done with the help of extraterrestrials or some kind of lost technology. Modern experts estimate that the building of Giza's Great Pyramid could have been completed by about 30,000 laborers within approximately 20 to 30 years. When considering the amount of time and resources required to complete projects and massive buildings in other civilizations, including our own modern society, it becomes clear that pyramid construction could have been, and was, undertaken and completed by human hands. Many medieval cathedrals took decades, even centuries, to complete – and these later projects were completed without slave labor.

The ancient Egyptians were master builders and utilized various quarries to extract the types of rock they needed to complete the pyramids. Rocks were hewn from gigantic slabs in the Aswan region and then conveyed along a slick surface to waiting barges. Scenes exist from antiquity depicting the process, in particular, a 19th-century B.C. carving of a lubricated slipway down which a giant statue is being dragged by four groups of men that total about 200.

The pyramids also once sat along a river route. While the Giza Plateau is now arid desert, researchers have found evidence of ancient seasonal waterways leading into key points at Giza that were used by barges to haul stones. As archaeologists continue to scour the area, the puzzle pieces begin to fall into place and create a clearer picture of who the pyramid builders were and how they did what they did.

In 1997, Egyptologist Mark Lehner set out to combine these hypotheses into a unified theory by making his own pyramid. His research grant was not generous enough to make a life-size replica, so he constructed a small-scale pyramid using a team of 12 men. Based on this model, he was not only able to calculate the manpower required for a project the size of the Great Pyramid, but he gained a valuable insight into how the process might have worked, from quarrying the stones by hand to pulling them along a slipway and setting them into place.

Needless to say, he did not quit his day job.

When the project was finished, Lehner used his calculations to scale the model upward to the size of the Great Pyramid. Learner's calculations determined that 1,200 men toiling every day could have quarried the amount of stone needed, while 2,000 men a day could have been employed to deliver the stone to the location. He worked with structural engineers to determine that over a period of 20 years, the total number of men needed to construct the pyramid would average out to around 5,000. Over the course of two decades, there would have been teams of men to support each other in service roles, amounting to around 30,000 in all.

Lehner's work was meticulous, and took into account many key factors such as modern vs. ancient tools, shipping methods, and engineering techniques. His project was by no means exact, since the match-up of ancient records to practical applications cannot be 100 percent precise, but it served to frame the scale of such a project within manageable parameters.

His research has led many to dismiss the concept that such an undertaking would have been impossible for the ancient Egyptians. On the contrary, as with many civilizations that followed, ambition has always seemed to test the limits of human capacity, from the Roman Coliseum to the Haghia Sophia church in Constantinople. To discount the Egyptians as "primitive" when they were capable of maintaining a work force over the span of decades dedicated to a single project would amount to a misunderstanding of human ingenuity in general. Therefore, the builders were not part of an advanced, lost civilization, but ordinary members of a society that was far more skilled and educated than the modern world gives it credit for.

So why were the pyramids built? The world's pyramid builders constructed their monuments for different reasons. The Egyptians built the world's largest pyramids as monuments to their god-kings, the pharaohs. The construction process usually coincided with the coronation of the pharaoh, who would assemble a team as one of his first duties of state. Some of the greatest engineers in history, along with teams of motivated and dedicated workers, architects, and artisans were mobilized. The great pyramids of Giza, built by three consecutive pharaohs in a dynasty beginning with the pharaoh Khufu, were thought to have taken their shape from myths of the sun god Ra, who created himself from a pyramid that represented the rays of the sun. Each pyramid was specifically oriented toward cardinal points and positioned facing the western horizon and the setting sun.

With great ceremony after his death, the pharaoh was mummified and entombed within the pyramid. Some experts believe that the specific engineering of the pyramids was designed to help resurrect pharaohs or lead them into the realm of the gods. They point to ingenious built-in shafts that usher star light through tiny cracks all the way into the burial chamber. From this, they hypothesize that the entire structure might serve to help guide the pharaoh into the hereafter, touched by the light of the stars.

The pyramids, though, were more than an incredibly elaborate cemetery. According to Egyptologist Peter Der Manuelian, these decorated tombs contained scenes of every aspect of life in ancient Egypt and extensive inscriptions written in an instructive style, making them a museum and even something of a primitive university. The tomb art includes depictions of ancient farmers working in their fields and tending livestock, fishing and fowling, costumes, carpentry, religious rituals, and burial practices.

The inscriptions and texts on the walls of the pyramids are the best-known examples of ancient Egyptian grammar and language. The writings on the tomb walls of Giza contain information on almost every aspect of Pharaonic civilization and were likely important tools of instruction in that society. These buildings show not only how the Egyptians died, but also how they lived.

Pyramids are not only found in Egypt. In Mesoamerica they served a variety of purposes. The majority of pyramids from Maya, Aztec, and other cultures were stepped and featured stairways leading to a flattened top. Often another small building would be set on top of the pyramid, in which kings could be interred or religious ceremonies could take place. These Mesoamerican pyramids were not just monuments to kings, but places of worship and religious activity.

Since the first outsider laid eyes on the Great Pyramids of Giza, people have been fascinated by the powerful symbolism behind these structures. Meticulously engineered and co-mingling religious ceremony with ingenious architecture and concepts of eternity, the world's pyramids have inspired everyone from archaeologists and scientists to New Age gurus. Their allegory is still as powerful today, as evidenced by their continued use as ornamental structures, from San Francisco's TransAmerica Building to the Pyramid Arena in Memphis, Tennessee (a town named after Egypt's ancient capital). They are a testament to the lasting power of ingenuity in an ancient culture.

Most of all, they are a testimony to the legacy that can be left behind by excellent craftsmanship. Its builders would have likely appreciated that today's onlookers of their handicraft believe that such a structure was so far beyond human ability that it required extraterrestrial assistance.

Chapter 5

Mycena (1900-1100 B.C.):
The Nemesis of Troy and Forerunner
to Classical Greek Civilization

Tales of Greek mythology have fueled the imaginations of students and literature lovers for generations, but over 100 years ago, a German businessman and archaeologist believed that they were more than just tales.

Instructed in the classical Greek epics that he fell in love with as a child, Heinrich Schliemann was convinced that Agamemnon really did return victorious from the mythical city of Troy to rule over all the citadels of Greece, only to later be murdered by his wife in the bathtub. Few people shared his belief – at the time, scholars considered *The Odyssey* and *The Iliad* to be nothing more than speculative fiction. In 1876 Schliemann set out to prove them wrong by retracing the steps of Greece's army in *The Iliad* and excavating a site he thought to be the king's final resting place.

Following a thorough excavation on the island of Crete, Schliemann eventually unearthed a tomb in the Bronze Age citadel of Mycenae. In that tomb, among many treasures, were three corpses. One still wore a gold death mask in the tradition of Mycenae, just as Homer described. Upon removing the mask, Schliemann found a remarkably preserved skull. Awed by his discovery, he said, "Today I have gazed upon the face of Agamemnon."

It is hard to take Schilemann at his word, considering that he committed enough strange acts in his life to merit a book of his own: that he destroyed the main layers of Troy by using dynamite during his excavation; that he divorced his first wife in order to marry a Greek schoolgirl, whom he selected through a marriage bureau and conditioned their nuptials on her being able to recite the *Iliad* from memory, and changing her name to Helen so that he could be married to his own Helen of Troy; that he intentionally falsified the dates of his findings so that they matched the times of the Trojan War; that he smuggled priceless antiquities out of Turkey at the dead of night on a ship – nevertheless, all of the controversy surrounding his life is overshadowed by him proving the historical reality of Homer's literature.

While modern archeologists have determined that the funeral mask dates to 1500 B.C., hundreds of years before Agamemnon's life as tradition regards it, legend and fact still appear to blend together seamlessly in the ancient citadel of Mycenae. Homer tells us that it was the seat of King Agamemnon, home to Menalaeus and Helen, and the mighty power that stood against Troy. Perseus is said to have been Mycenae's first king, initiating a long line of Perseid rulers. Homer's details are copious, describing royal families, lineages, and military exploits.

Whether there is truth in his accounts is the subject of debate because he wrote at a time when Mycenae lay in ruin - a time after what has come to be known as the Bronze Age Collapse that led to a dark age throughout Greece. It was oral tradition that carried the stories of Mycenae to Homer 400 years later, which could easily have been exaggerated by centuries of telling and retelling, fortifying, and re-imagining.

Still, archaeologists like Schliemann have unearthed artifacts, tombs, and opulent palaces that seem to correspond with Homer's heroic tales. Details of the palace at Mycenae fit well with the blind poet's description of Agamemnon's home. Could there have been a real Agamemnon? A real Perseus?

Mycenae is generally understood to have been settled around 2000 B.C., but pottery shards have been found dating from a thousand years earlier, making it an early Bronze Age site among the earliest settlements in the region and a contemporary of the Minoans of Crete. It is not known whether the Mycenaeans displaced an older Neolithic culture that occupied the site 6,000 years ago, or whether they themselves simply began to reach out to other ancient cultures and expand their knowledge, eventually evolving into one of the ancient world's most influential civilizations.

No one is certain as to the origins of the Mycenaeans. The word "Mycenae" has no meaning in Greek, and the language from which the word derives is as yet unknown. Whether or not the Mycenaeans were originally Indo-European nomads or the remnant of some ancient indigenous Neolithic tribe, over the course of 700 years they would come to exemplify the essence of Greek culture, as it is their memory that is preserved in Homer's epics.

They have left behind writings in the form of Mycenaean Greek, the most ancient attested form of the language. They wrote in a script called Linear B, a syllabic script that uses ideographic signs and is closer to Egyptian hieroglyphs than the ancient Greek alphabet. The language was not deciphered until Michael Ventris accomplished the task and unlocked the language in 1952. Unfortunately, the texts available say much about the society but little about its culture. Of the 6,000 tablets and potsherds that have been recovered, most are financial lists and inventories rather than any poetry or prose.

From 2000 to 1700 B.C., Mycenaean power and influence grew dramatically through conquest rather than trade, as was the traditional means of expansion among the sea-faring peoples of the Mediterranean. This can be seen in the surviving Mycenaean forts, which date back to 1600 B.C. and are the world's oldest surviving structures of its kind. Their expansion throughout the Peloponnese was influenced by interaction with the older Minoan culture of Crete and was marked by the construction of fortified citadels. They adapted their own language to reflect this Minoan influence, developing a hybrid language of Mycenaean Greek.

According to Mycenaean tablets, the collection of city-states represented a well-organized sociopolitical entity, with a king at its center and a feudal-style structure that provided goods, services, and manpower for the fortification of the citadels. Each citadel was accessed by means of a corbel-arched corridor and enclosed wells, storage rooms, and land that was used for grazing and farming. Mycenaean artisans and farmers were renowned throughout the Mediterranean region by the 16th-century B.C., creating sophisticated pottery and sculptures; state-of-the-art weaponry; and high-quality olive oil, wine, and agricultural products.

By 1350 B.C., Mycenae was the central power in Southern Greece. All major Greek cities, from Thebes and Athens to Argos and Pylos, were monuments to the glory of Mycenae. The city of Mycenae itself was built on a hilltop overlooking suburbs and small villages in the surrounding lowlands. The gargantuan acropolis and other buildings of Mycenae's urban centers were constructed with uncannily large and heavy stones -- so large that they earned the name "cyclopean" from ancient onlookers. The Hellenic Greeks marveled at the palaces and tombs of Mycenae, fortified by these mammoth blocks of limestone, 20-feet thick and 40-feet tall, and concluded that they could only have been built with the help of the one-eyed giants.

The cyclopean fortifications of Mycenaean citadels provided protection from enemies, a necessity due to their militaristic nature. As a people bent on conquest, the Mycenaeans, now masters of Peloponnesian Greece and the Aegean Sea, looked beyond their horizon and set out to expand their power. Their battles and conquests eventually led them to the Minoan stronghold of Crete.

Despite, or perhaps because of, the conquest of Crete, the influence of the Minoans on Mycenae can be seen in everything from their writing to their pottery, art, architecture, and religion. The Mycenaeans were intelligent and organized, and gradually adopted Minoan customs with a decidedly Mycenaean accent. With the conquest of this major Mediterranean power, the Mycenaeans became the inspiration for Hellenic Greece in art, architecture, and mythology. The Greeks, as Homer's stories indicate, revered Mycenae as the progenitor of their own civilization, and therefore combined myth with reality and narrated the story of one the most influential civilizations that humanity has ever known.

The Mycenaeans built their fortified citadels in strategic locations using advanced architecture and engineering. Their architects made particular use of the corbel arch – a state-of-the-art weight-bearing structure of the time – in their galleries, halls, and labyrinthine "beehive" tombs. The broad, rectangular king's hall, or "megaron", found in every Mycenaean citadel was the precursor in design to the classic temples of Greece such as the Parthenon and the temples of Zeus and Apollo.

As their power and influence grew, so did the infrastructure of their society and the need to support a growing population. The Mycenaeans answered this need with remarkable achievements of engineering. They built massive stone bridges using successive layers of smaller and larger rocks to create structural reinforcement. These bridges connected the Mycenaean highways and reduced the difficulty and time requirement for travel, facilitating access to trade routes throughout the Peloponnese. They created reservoirs by building dams with the cyclopean blocks and dug out canals to divert lake water, both minimizing flood damage and providing a regular source of irrigation for their crops.

While the Mycenaeans may have been a militaristic people, they were also keenly aware of aesthetics and quality of life. The walls and floors of their megarons were adorned with elaborate frescoes, and their city gates were carved with ornate heraldry. The influence of Minoan culture on Mycenae can be seen in the many artifacts recovered from Mycenaean tombs. Beautiful carvings in silver and gold, from busts to statuary, accompanied heroes on their journey to the afterlife. The swords and weaponry the Mycenaeans wrought were meticulously engraved and decorated. Jewelry, pottery, and weapons produced by Mycenaeans were widely sought after and have been found in sites as distant as Georgia, England, and Ireland. These discoveries indicate the broad extent of Mycenae's cultural influence across the European continent. Along with Egypt and Anatolia, Mycenae was at the height of Bronze Age civilization in the Mediterranean.

The principle question surrounding Mycenaean culture, however, is not about pottery, architecture, or citadels. It is whether or not this civilization was actually one of the two armies that fought in the Trojan War, and if so, how much the Trojan War resembled the events as described in the *Iliad*. The answer? As always with events thousands of years in the past, it is difficult to say. According to Manfred Korfmann, director of excavations at Troy, there were likely several armed conflicts in and around Troy at the end of the Late Bronze Age, but we cannot know whether some or all of these conflicts were distilled into later memory and recounted by Homer in the eighth century.

He is, however, cautiously optimistic. "If someone came up to me at the excavation [of Troy] one day and expressed his or her belief that the Trojan War did indeed happen here, my response as an archaeologist working at Troy would be: Why not?"

As Schliemann discovered over 100 years ago, one can visit Troy today in modern-day Turkey and recognize the general outlines of places where the action happened from descriptions in the *Iliad*, such as where soldiers climbed up a slope to a sanctuary in "holy Ilios" – the most repeated epithet in the *Iliad*. If nothing else, the archeological excavation of the city suggests that in 1300 B.C., the city was of considerable size and wealth. It would have been worth it for the Mycenaeans to attempt to conquer and plunder Troy for its riches and for its importance in controlling access from the Mediterranean to the Black Sea and from Asia Minor to southeastern Europe. The ancient Greeks appreciated the importance of strategic forts and would not have minded controlling the greatest fort in the region.

Even if the ancient Mycenaeans truly did win the Trojan War, the future was not bright for the victors. Seemingly at the height of its power and influence in 1200 B.C., Mycenae abruptly vanished. Evidence shows that the cities of southern Greece, including the citadel of Mycenae itself, were burned around the same time period and quickly abandoned. Surviving Mycenaeans are thought to have fled to regions that were once Mycenaean colonies. There, they blended with the local cultures, assimilated, and their language and customs disappeared over time.

The cause of the Mycenaean decline is not fully understood and has led to many theories. Some scholars note that earthquakes riddled the seismically active Greek mainland and could have easily leveled their capital, but this fails to explain such an abrupt disappearance. Others have sought evidence to corroborate ancient Greek historical accounts of an invasion by the descendants of Heracles. Ongoing investigation could eventually lend some weight to this theory – at least the invasion part, not the part about the invaders being descendants of a demigod – just as Heinrich Schliemann's discoveries of Troy and Mycenae brought to light the facts surrounding the legend. Nevertheless, despite nearly two centuries of study, this "Dorian" invasion remains a myth.

An expanded view of the Mediterranean world beyond Mycenae reveals a large-scale decline nearly as abrupt as the Mycenaean abandonment, which affected not only Greece but the Hittite civilization, Syria, and the New Kingdom of Egypt. During this period, known as the "Bronze Age Collapse", cities throughout the Mediterranean region were mysteriously abandoned and trade routes disrupted. In short, the region's Bronze Age civilizations seem to have collapsed all at once, and then plunged into a dark age that lasted centuries.

Explanations for the Bronze Age Collapse range from climate change to invasions of iron weapon-wielding barbarians. Evidence does exist, however, for a dark age among the Greeks. Out of this period of isolation and barbarism emerged classical Greece, an astounding civilization that gave rise to modern concepts of democracy, produced the world's most renowned philosophers, and allowed Homer to capture on papyrus the stories of the heroes and kings of a forgotten empire.

Yet even though the Mycenaeans may not have produced the literary culture that their descendants did, it was their mythical deeds that became the stuff of ancient Greek fiction. We recount their bravery today in schools across the world and associate the word "epic" with such Mycenaean figures as Achilles, Agamemnon, and Odysseus. Their civilization mysteriously collapsed, but their legacy reverberates through history.

Chapter 6

Ancient American Explorers (500 B.C. – 1500 A.D.): The Unknown Adventurers Who Arrived a Millennium Before Columbus

The reputation of Christopher Columbus has taken a beating in recent years. Once an icon of fearless exploration in the face of the horror of falling off the edge of the earth, and a symbol of Italian-American pride, he has become a byword in some circles for exploitation. Every Columbus Day, post-colonial researchers point out the atrocities committed by Columbus upon his arrival to the New World. He massacred the native population, stole their gold, and enslaved their women. From their perspective, his discovery of America is analogous to what Matthew Inman describes as asteroids discovering the dinosaurs 65 million years ago.

Other figures, such as leftist historian Howard Zinn, go one step further and call him the father of the Atlantic slave trade. While it is difficult to blame him for constructing a system that didn't crystalize until after his death, there are plenty of reasons to believe that even his contemporaries found his behavior deplorable. According to a 48-page report written in 1500, he governed Hispaniola by torture and mutilation, often cracking down on native uprisings through painful executions. Upon the testimony of 23 men, the Spanish court of Isabella and Ferdinand - the instigators of the Spanish Inquisition - ordered him back to Spain in chains and had him imprisoned. He was eventually released, but his governorship in the New World was revoked. He spent the remaining years of his life in penury, still believing that he had discovered a shorter route to India.

All of these historical criticisms tear down his image, but they have not deprived him of what is thought to be his chief accomplishment. Columbus was the first European to visit the New World and successfully bring back the news, thus opening up the Western Hemisphere for colonization from the Old World. Vikings may have arrived to Canada centuries earlier, but Columbus' claim to fame was that he stayed.

However, new findings by researchers suggest that Columbus may not even have this accomplishment to hang his tricorn hat on. Archeological findings in the New World have turned up several surprises that show the morally-compromised Italian may not have even been the first to visit the Americas and return home to tell the tale.

Evidence of ancient cultures paying visits to the New World and possibly staying are nothing short of mind-boggling. According to author Stephen Wagner, material remains left behind include a coin from the Greek city-state of Syracuse dating from 490 B.C. found in Alabama in 1957; a coin of Antiochus IV, king of Syria from 175 to 164 B.C., found in 1882 in Cass County, Illinois; the 1914 discovery of Egyptian statuettes of Osiris and Isis that were found in Mayan ruins; and the 1886 discovery of a shipwreck in Galveston Bay, Texas whose construction was typically Roman.

Most interesting is an inscription found in Brazil that is thought to derive from the Phoenician culture - a pagan, Semitic culture that practiced human sacrifice and reached its apogee 2,500-3,000 years prior. Doubts about its authenticity exist, but some have claimed it to be genuine, such as the iconoclastic Near Eastern scholar Cyrus Gordon. The inscription reads: "We are sons of Canaan from Sidon, the city of the king. Commerce has cast us on this distant shore, a land of mountains. We [sacrificed] a youth for the exalted gods and goddesses in the nineteenth year of Hiram, our mighty king... We were at sea together for two years around the land belonging to Ham [Africa] but were separated by a storm ['from the hand of Baal'], and we were no longer with our companions. So we have come here, twelve men and three women, on a... shore which I, the Admiral, control. But auspiciously may the gods and goddesses favor us!"

The idea that ancient cultures visited the Americas and may have established themselves is a significant challenge to conventional wisdom. Such ideas were once dismissed as fringe theories or articles of religious faith. A tenet of Mormon history, for example, holds that the lost tribes of Israel escaped captivity from the Assyrians and traveled to the New World, where they were the forefathers of today's American Indians.

The most widely accepted theory of colonization of the Western Hemisphere among Neolithic archeologists holds that, 13,000 to 15,000 years ago, the Ice Age's effects on environmental conditions provided access to the Americas for nomadic Siberian and Asian peoples. They crossed the Bering Strait via a land bridge and descended southward to populate the land, moving from the west toward the south and east. They brought with them new technology in the form of the Clovis point, a flat, sharp spear head that was used in hunting, carving, and cutting, and was essential to survival in the Pleistocene and Holocene epochs.

The question remains, were these shores visited by others before the Europeans? Did ancient sea powers embark on heroic voyages now long forgotten? A growing body of evidence of the influence of foreign cultures in the New World is mounting as scholars and scientists unearth evidence of historical events that sometimes defy explanation.

One hypothesis is the Solutrean Theory, which argues that a European ethnic group may be the forefathers of many of the native populations of the Americas. This theory's name refers to a Neolithic people who occupied ancient Portugal, Spain, and France. Long before Columbus sailed to the Americas, even before ancient Egypt, Greece, and Rome, the Solutreans may have set out to explore the west through primitive oceanic vessels.

Discoveries at Tighman Island, Maryland and sites in Virginia and Pennsylvania in the early 21st Century, showed Clovis tools and spear heads found there to be much older than those found in Clovis, New Mexico in 1929. Researchers thus began rethinking the origin of Native Americans. The

Clovis artifacts from New Mexico, thought to be the oldest, were younger than those found at Tighman by 5,000 years.

Clovis tools from 20,000-year-old European Solutrean sites closely match those on the American east coast, whereas there is almost no evidence of the same tools along the northern Bering Strait route. Researchers theorize that the ancestors of eastern Native Americans may in fact have been hunters who migrated across the Atlantic from Europe 20,000 years ago in search of game. The Ice Age terrain was different: a large ice cap extended far south into the Atlantic Ocean. Less water meant shallower seas and more islands. It is therefore plausible that the Solutreans could have paddled along the ice cap and island-hopped their way to what is now the east coast of America.

If this theory is true, what does it mean for Columbus's 1492 discovery? First, it still shows that the Europeans discovered America, but also that Columbus's own ancient ancestors first laid claim to the land that he stumbled upon 21,000 years later.

A second popular hypothesis is the Polynesian Diaspora theory. The idea is that Polynesians visited the shores of South America and possibly North America, a notion that is hard to discount based on the impressive seafaring abilities of the Pacific society. Based on genetic testing, islanders used somewhat primitive boats to routinely cross hundreds of miles of deep water to trade with islands in their vicinity. While there may not have been permanent settlements, there were numerous interactions between Ancient Americans and the Polynesians who explored the South Pacific over a period of 900 years, long before any records of European sea exploration.

One piece of evidence for such a theory comes from the humble sweet potato. It was a favored staple crop of South Pacific islanders for over 1,000 years, and it originates in the Americas. How this vegetable spread throughout the South Pacific is the subject of much debate. Some scholars say that the South Americans sailed from their own shores to outposts like Easter Island and interacted with the natives. Others say that it was the islanders who discovered the western shores of South America and took the potatoes with them.

Easter Island itself has been the subject of genetic studies that may link native islander DNA with that of mainland South Americans. Mocha Island, off the coast of Chile, may have been one of the places where interaction between mainlanders and Pacific Islanders was an everyday occurrence. Forthcoming archeological excavations and genetic studies aim to uncover evidence of that interaction.

Other theories about ancient colonizers concern the Ancient Copper Mines of Isla Royal. Mystery surrounds this island located in northern Lake Superior. Here, copper mines have been found dating back some 6,000 years, well before the beginning of the Bronze Age, which was inaugurated in 2,000 B.C. due to the proliferation of the eponymous metal. The mine pits were discovered in the 1840s when modern mine operations sought to exploit the vast amount of copper in the region. Some of these ancient pits were as deep as 20 feet. Excavations of awls, spuds, spear heads, and even caches of unworked copper indicate that the region was mined regularly, possibly as long as thousands of years by some estimates. The identity of those who mined this site and the destination of all that copper remain a mystery.

Estimates of the amount of copper extracted from the Isle Royale mines vary wildly, but everyone from pseudo-scientists to archaeologists agree that judging from the range of mining activity and the large number of mines, a disparity clearly exists between the amount of copper found to date and the estimated amount that was extracted. How these Stone Age miners knew how to identify copper and why they mined it has been the subject of much scholarly discussion.

Could it be that the Isle Royale miners had contact with other Bronze Age or Copper Age civilizations? It is plausible to believe so, but there is not enough evidence to either support or deny such a hypothesis. Copper artifacts found in the region attest to the fact that the early Isle Royale miners worked with copper, and mining techniques from the British Isles show striking similarities to theirs.

Over 3,000 years ago, the ancestors of coastal Europeans may have traded with and learned from Native American miners. The end of the Bronze Age roughly coincides with the end of the first phase of copper mining in Isle Royale around 1200 B.C. – a coincidence that might point to the end of a once lucrative trade economy that could have spanned oceans in the ancient world.

Of course, no discussion about early visitors to America is complete without mentioning China. It was the wealthiest, most technologically advanced civilization in the world until a few hundred years ago, and hugged the Pacific Ocean; many researchers are in fact baffled that China did *not* colonize the Western hemisphere. Whatever happened in the past, it was not for a want of trying. Roughly 1,500 years ago, a Buddhist missionary expedition led by Hui Shen claimed to have discovered the mythical land of Fusang. Many literary scholars have posited that the Chinese reckoning of distance at the time places Hui Shen's Fusang on the California coast. Whether or not that account is true and the Chinese did sail so far afield, there is other puzzling evidence of Chinese influence in pre-Columbian America.

As early as the Xia Dynasty, around 2000 B.C., bamboo annals recount Chinese sea voyages. If the ancient Polynesians were capable of trans-oceanic voyages, certainly a power as organized and advanced as ancient China could have mounted a similar expedition.

The most radical theory of China's discovery of the New World comes from a 2002 book by Gavin Menzies called "1421: The Year China Discovered America." In the book, he argues that from 1421 to 1423, during the Ming Dynasty, the fleets of Admiral Zheng undertook such a trip. The legendary admiral led seven epic voyages as far west as Africa, and his ships were so massive that all the ships of Columbus and Vasco de Gama could have fit on a single deck of a single vessel of his fleet. Menzies argues that Zheng discovered Australia, New Zealand, the Americas, Antarctica, and the Northeast Passage, even circumnavigating Greenland. The discoveries were only lost because the Mandarin bureaucrats of the Imperial court refused to continue funding the expensive adventures. His theory has been almost universally panned by Sinologists for faulty uses of sources, but what is known for sure is why China did *not* succeed. When Emperor Zhu Di died in 1424, the new emperor forbade further explorations, ending China's chances for colonization of the New World once and for all.

Yet, some believe that China could have been a progenitor of civilizations in the New World. In Mexico, Olmec culture preceded all other Mesoamerican cultures and was a highly advanced civilization that existed between 1500 and 400 B.C. Olmec architecture, culture, and art informed later Mexican and Central American civilizations, but the Olmec themselves seem to have emerged without precedent. Could it have been Chinese influence that inspired the Olmec to carve out the fundamentals of Mesoamerican architecture, craftsmanship, and design from the surrounding jungle?

Olmec art is characterized first and foremost by faces. "Colossal Heads" were an Olmec trademark, but finer and smaller items were also created by skilled Olmec artisans. Among these – and often identified as evidence of Chinese influence – is a jade mask that strikingly resembles Bronze Age Chinese masks, and a figurine depicting a wrestler who appears to be sitting in lotus position and sports distinctly Chinese facial features. A pair of scholars also claim to have found celts – special tools used primarily for ritual ceremonies – inscribed with Chinese characters in Olmec plots.

If the Chinese visited, though, where is the DNA evidence? Why did they not stay and enter into an economic relationship with these Mesoamericans? Some scholars point to genealogical similarities between Asian, Mediterranean, and Mesoamerican DNA. In addition, certain written characters and linguistic traits between Chinese and the Olmec language, implausible as it may seem, show uncanny similarities.

These tidbits of information indicate a possible relationship between China and the Olmec civilization in the pre-Columbian era, though researchers continue to argue on both sides of the debate. Regardless of whether there was a trade relationship between the two ancient civilizations, it disappeared long before the advent of modern maritime exploration, and an explanation for that disappearance may never be uncovered.

Ancient civilizations in the Americas are among the world's most mysterious. They are rife with characteristics that defy explanation, and just as mysterious is their disappearance. The theories of foreign peoples influencing early American settlements often provides a logical explanation for a set of circumstances that otherwise might be difficult to explain. How and why would Stone Age tribesmen develop a large-scale mining operation? How could legends, indigenous foodstuffs, art, and architecture share so many uncanny similarities with foreign cultures if they developed in isolated regions? Questions like these often raise even more perplexing questions, and the answers are sure to lie somewhere in between.

The answers to these questions, if nothing else, may further reduce the legacy of Christopher Columbus. They are enough to make the once universally-beloved explorer roll in his grave. Still, at the very least, the Italian navigator will always have two inalienable accomplishments to console his woes: a federal holiday in his name, and a capital city in Ohio.

Chapter 7

The Ancient Pueblo peoples (1200 B.C.):
The Ancient Rock Climbers of the American Southwest

In 1539, Spanish explorer Francisco Vázquez de Coronado was named governor of the kingdom of Nueva Galica, located in today's American Southwest. The conquistador had grand ambitions in the New World, most importantly to conquer the mythical Seven Cities of Gold. However, acquiring those limitless riches would have to wait as he set out to conquer a more immediate issue – his afternoon lunch. Before he could sit down to eat, Coronado was interrupted by a visit from a Franciscan friar, the same man he had dispatched to explore the areas north of modern-day Texas. The friar told his Excellency that he had been to the mythical golden city of Cibola, a place of vast wealth where buildings occupied cliffs and high hills in an area as large as Mexico City.

Coronado immediately assembled an expedition. His imagination ran wild with dreams of the never-ending supplies of gold that would adorn the city. The young commander had every reasonable expectation to strike it rich, as he had heard tales from his fellow conquistadors about the massive fortunes held by the Indian civilizations. When Hernán Cortés and his troops first visited the Aztec capital of Tenochtitlán in 1519, they were immediately gifted with gold from Montezuma II. In the markets, they observed untold numbers of precious stones being bought and sold, and these same soldiers acquired all of this wealth with their conquest of the city in 1521.

He was particularly interested in the story of the ransom of the Incan emperor. In 1532, 160 conquistadors captured Emperor Atahualpa, the last sovereign ruler of the South American empire before the Spanish conquest. To obtain his freedom, he paid his gold-hungry captors a ransom that is widely considered to be the largest in history: he filled a room with gold and then twice over with silver. The room was 22 feet long by 17 feet wide, and filled to a height of 8 feet (or 6.7 meters by 5.17 meters, up to 2.45 meters). It totaled over 13,000 pounds of gold and twice as much silver. The gold was divided up among the captors and each of the 160 men received the equivalent of $500,000 in today's currency. The leader, Francisco Pizzaro, received 14 times as much – or $7 million.

To his infinite disappointment, Coronado found nothing of the sort when he reached his destination. He found only traces of the friar's mythical boasts. Stepping deep into a narrow canyon, Coronado saw abandoned dwellings carved into the rock face. The facades held rows of mud-and-stone structures that soared 600 feet above the canyon floor. They were echoes of an ancient golden age, buried by time and haunted by the mysterious disappearance of its owners.

He was astonished at the settlements built high in the cliffs. They were spaced apart from each other horizontally and vertically, requiring expert-level mountaineering and sheer rock wall climbing ability to move around the town. What powers did this civilization possess that could allow them to live comfortably in such an inaccessible environment?

Long before the Europeans arrived in North America, an advanced civilization existed in what is now the Four Corners region of Utah, New Mexico, Colorado, and Arizona. Great cities flourished among the sandstone cliffs and once fertile canyon lands. Astronomers and engineers analyzed the stars and built great roadways, towers, and stone complexes, some of which even today evade attempts at rational explanation. These remnants are the monuments of the Ancient Pueblo peoples, formerly known as the Anasazi – which has come to mean "ancient people" but is actually a Navajo word for "enemy ancestors."

The greatest architectural accomplishment of this vanished civilization was the houses and settlements built into the sheer rock wall of the Chaco Canyon in western New

Mexico. The 30,000-square-mile landscape of canyons, buttes, and mesas housed a population of 30,000 at its peak. There they built such villages as the Pueblo Bonito, which at certain areas was as high as five stories and contained 800 rooms. This village was part of a network of settlements connected by a 400-mile system of roads, some as wide as 30 feet, flanked along the way by astronomical observatories.

Today, various American Indian tribes of the region claim to be descendants of the Ancient Pueblo peoples and call themselves the Puebloans. They believe that the Anasazi did not disappear, but rather evolved into today's American Indian population of the Southwest. Their evidence is an oral tradition whose connection to the past is, they maintain, an artifact of the Puebloan golden age that is every bit as reliable a piece of evidence as the archeological remains of a lost city or an ancient manuscript. While the answer to the mystery of why the Puebloans abandoned their great cities may be contained within the tribes' oral traditions, archaeologists have looked to the beautifully preserved buildings and artifacts in this arid region for additional clues.

The earliest records of corn cultivation in the Four Corners region date back to 1500 B.C. Over the next two millennia, the inhabitants of this area became experts at dry farming, relying on weather conditions to provide water for their crops. Eventually, they developed simple irrigation systems by diverting runoff from smaller streams and building dams to maintain productivity. They were aware of the dangers of soil erosion and over-farming, thus preventing the soil from becoming depleted.

The ancient Puebloan culture was not a homogenous culture but rather a confederacy of customs and peoples, each of which contributed to the civilization as a whole. Three major branches of the culture have been recognized according to their location – in Chaco Canyon of northwest New Mexico, Kayenta of northeast Arizona, and Northern San Juan in southwestern Colorado. In these three locales, researchers have found different artifacts that share certain key characteristics. Most notable was the Puebloans' communal architectural style, farming techniques, and pottery. They were able to build up their society and infrastructure due to living in relative peace for over 1,000 years. Their society was mostly egalitarian and dependent on farming, hunting, and gathering.

Around 750 B.C., the Puebloans began to develop sophisticated building techniques and an advanced level of art and design. Their cities grew in stature and influence throughout the region. Puebloan culture can be recognized by its distinctive architectural accent, from circular "observatories" to stone brick cliff towers and vast networks of apartments carved directly into sandstone cliff-sides. These structures remained the largest buildings in North America until the 19th century.

The 150 years between 900 and 1150 A.D. is considered the Puebloan "Golden Age," when the civilization reached its zenith in urban design and social development. It was during this period that the Great Houses of Chaco Canyon were built and the distinctive cliff dwellings of Mesa Verde and Bandelier National Monument were carved out of the sandstone or erected with stone masonry and cemented with mortar. Some apartment complexes in Chaco Canyon held hundreds of rooms and accommodated large numbers of families. Cliff overhangs that had developed naturally through eons of erosion into dramatic water and wind-swept formations hid Puebloan dwellings. They were camouflaged as rock and reached towering heights.

Walking along the ledges of the ruins is enough to give a tourist vertigo, particularly as they try to imagine an entire city functioning at such a precarious location with seemingly unscalable cliffs. From the vantage point of the tourist trails, there are ruins that are inaccessible without ropes or climbing equipment. Reaching certain dwellings would require serious mountaineering experience, even with the benefit of such equipment.

David Roberts wrote an account of the site in the Smithsonian magazine and attempted to explain how a civilization that was essentially built on a rock climbing wall could operate. One theory holds that the Ancient Pueblo peoples clambered up felled tree trunks notched by stone axes that formed tiny footholds. The hundreds of niches created a system of log ladders on ledges hundreds of feet above the ground. Such an arrangement suggests an entire society of rock climbers, in which even its elderly citizens would likely be able to show up at a modern-day university recreation center climbing wall and easily best the heartiest of students.

This explanation still boggles the mind. One wrong step would mean falling hundreds of feet to the canyon floor, almost ensuring instant death. It is difficult to imagine the elderly, small children, or entire families carelessly walking along paths that are directly parallel to sheer drop-offs. Yet not only is that how the city is constructed, but it includes all the trappings of an ancient cosmopolitan center. The masoned dwellings held granaries, temples, and mansions.

The inhabitants may have courted death every day, but they took care to add aesthetic beauty to their homes. The outer walls were plastered with a coat of mud and the facades were painted white. Lines and hatching patterns were then incised into the plaster. This all helped to create tonal differences.

Nevertheless, the most important aspect of the settlements located high in the cliffs is that they offered defense and protection due to the stone overhangs and their inaccessibility. Protection meant social stability, and stability meant development. As a result, these major urban centers accommodated increasing numbers of people, and supported influxes of religious pilgrims, tourists, and tradesmen who came from surrounding cultures.

Great roads were built to connect cities or led to scenic features, such as hilltop overlooks, or practical locations like freshwater springs. Some roads, in particular the "Great Road," simply led out of the canyons with no particular identifiable destination. These roads were originally thought to have been provided for easy mobility of standing armies, but no evidence of permanent armies in the Puebloan communities has yet been found. The roads probably also served to support the Puebloan economy. There is evidence to support this, since trade items from cultures as far away as

Mexico have been found in Puebloan cities. Cotton from the south was used in the weaving of textiles, and shells, along with coral and other precious coastal items, were used in Puebloan jewelry, combs, and hairpins.

In the ancient culture, religion and craftsmanship appear to have mixed together. Approximately every 60 rooms in a typical golden age Puebloan complex featured what is known as a kiva – usually a circular room or multi-floored tower that was used for industrial purposes like weaving, as well as ceremonial purposes associated with the kachina belief system. This system is still understood and practiced by local descendants of Puebloan culture, such as the Hopi, Ute, Zuni, and Navajo, and kivas are still used today for ritual purposes. Some of the ancient kivas were massive, and one of the largest is the Great Kiva at the Aztec Ruins National Monument, which features 15 top rooms, each with an exterior door. The pillars of the kiva rest on immense stone disks that were hauled from quarries many miles away.

Evidence uncovered in Chaco Canyon indicates that the Puebloans were also dedicated astronomers. Ceremonial buildings in Chaco Canyon, including large kivas, were clearly oriented to capture astronomical cycles of the sun, moon, and stars. This indicates that the Puebloans were keenly aware of their surroundings and possessed an intellectual capacity and curiosity that places them on a level equal to the classical Greek, Roman, and Abbasid civilizations.

Many archaeo-astronomy scholars have identified Chaco Canyon as the ceremonial center of a complex of buildings aligned to reflect the trajectory of heavenly bodies during specific seasons. If this is the case, it is likely that pilgrimages from astronomers of other cultures throughout the Americas would have existed, and these cultures would have shared knowledge of their ancient religion and science. This growing network of shared knowledge may have contributed significantly to the growth of the Ancient Pueblo peoples during its golden age.

The unique architecture of the Puebloans reflected shrewd urban planning that was conducted over long periods of time. By the 12th century A.D., however, massive migrations resulted in abandonment and new cities established at higher altitudes. Scholars are puzzled by these late-period migrations from the canyons to higher elevations where farming was more difficult. Some have hypothesized that the higher elevations afforded residents protection from aggressive attacks, indicating that the cliff dwelling Puebloans may have been the target of increasing aggression. Isolated in the highlands, they may have resorted to cannibalism to survive, but evidence of large-scale warfare and cannibalism are the subjects of intense debate. If they did exist, they are not likely the main reason for the Puebloan migrations.

Environmental clues tell a story of successive droughts in the region, though the Puebloans managed to survive drought many times through their centuries-long inhabitation of the cliffs. During their golden age, however, more people occupied the cities than at any other time in Puebloan history. According to tree ring data, the period between 1125 and 1270 was a time of severe drought. This cycle of dry weather might have been the "perfect storm" of environmental issues, since there were not one but three successive droughts over the relatively short span of 100 years. This, combined with possible deforestation associated with population growth, may have been a key contributor to the Puebloans' disappearance. Indeed, each of the successive drought periods – the 10th, 12th, and 13th centuries A.D., respectively – corresponds with shifts in the pattern of Puebloan settlement, away from their homeland and into areas that created new challenges.

Could it be that the Puebloans were simply victims of their own success? Population growth supported by a successful, safe, and sustainable way of life had reached its height by the 12th century. There is even evidence that people from other cultures may have moved to the great Puebloan cities. This could have exacerbated all the other factors associated with the Puebloans' disappearance. Deforestation from the construction of ever-expanding dwellings, the shortage of tillable land in proportion to the ever-increasing population, and the devastating cycle of ever-lengthening droughts (the last, in 1275, lasting 14 years) could all have contributed to increased aggression, migration, starvation, and eventually, abandonment.

Another possibility is that the Ancient Pueblo peoples were authors of their own demise. According to archeologist Stephen Leksen, the society was slowly torn apart by long-lasting violence. In order to quell potential uprisings, the government ordered goon squads to commit executions against social outcasts and cannibalized them. This was a means of social control that put the Anasazi in a constant state of fear. It created paranoia that made villages turn on each other. They formed alliances and attempted to crush any opponents before they were crushed first. This persisted into the Spanish period, and as late as 1700, Hopi villages attacked the Hopi pueblo of Awatovi, setting fire to the houses, killing all of the adult males, enslaving the women and children, and cannibalizing the victims.

In contrast to the prevailing theory that the cliff dwellings appear to have been abandoned, the Puebloan people insist that they never truly abandoned their ancient homeland. They claim that, even today, they still make pilgrimages to the cities, and their oral tradition lives within the culture of their people. Just as the Mayas still live and work in the jungles and coastal areas of Central America and speak their ancient language, so the diversity of cultures that once occupied North America's biggest cities still continues on in its ancient philosophies, languages, and rich oral tradition.

Nevertheless, the Puebloans of today claiming direct ancestry to a lost civilization can strike as a bit strange, similar to a gelato shop owner in Italy claiming himself to be a modern-day Roman, or a tire salesman in Iran thinking of himself as a direct descendant of King Darius. Still, however odd it appears to modern Westerners, there is an important lesson to be learned from the Puebloans' sentimental connection to the past. Whenever it appears that a society vanished into thin air, it is often times equally as plausible that it merely evolved or mutated into a modern culture that we know of today.

Chapter 8

The Nabataeans (37-100 A.D.): The Lost Civilization that Mystified Indiana Jones

The ancient stone city of Petra in modern-day Jordan was once the seat of the powerful Hellenistic civilization of the Nabataea. Its magnificent architecture and ceramics were the by-products of a trade powerhouse that dominated a region between Arabia and Syria, from the Euphrates to the Red Sea. For today's tourists, though, the lost city holds importance for an entirely different reason.

"That's the temple from Indiana Jones and the Last Crusades, isn't it?"

The exclamation is uttered hundreds of times a day by Westerners awestruck when they emerge from a narrow passageway and first look upon the incredible rock-cut facade of Khazneh. They see the famous temple that formed the backdrop of the beloved film from their childhood, among George Lucas's final creative endeavors, before he set out to ruin the franchise with "Indiana Jones and the Kingdom of the Crystal Skull." Sight of the temple immediately triggers memories from the film's climactic scene in which Indy and his father, played by Sean Connery, narrowly escape the temple as it crashes down on his Nazi adversaries.

The temple of Khazneh is seen during the final part of the tour of the lost city, and it is quite breathtaking. Khazneh truly feels like a lost city because, in order to access it, one must pass through the final bend of a narrow canyon. They are then confronted by the towering rock facade that is heavily ornamented with Greek-style columns. With nothing but desert rockscape surrounding it, the temple appears to have been dropped from the skies.

The marvelous architecture is befitting to the backdrop of Indiana Jones, a character who loved to plumb the depths of lost civilizations—and what a civilization Nabataea was. At its height, the society stretched from Israel and Jordan to the Arab peninsula. From 312 B.C. to 106 A.D., the Nabataeans astounded their neighbors with their accomplishments in engineering, art, and architecture. Such public works were funded by a loosely controlled trading network, which knitted together the societies surrounding the Arabian Desert by controlling the oases used by desert-traversing caravans. They were fed by agriculture packed into the limited fertile lands. The civilization had no clearly defined boundaries, making it able to absorb the elements of its neighbors, but also making it susceptible to conquest by powerful empires.

Therefore, it is more appropriate to compare it to Coca-Cola than a fully-formed state. Much like the soda corporation – which, with its massive wealth, can fund the Olympics and construct massive football stadiums – it was capable of producing wonderful works but did not employ a permanent army or attempt to manage the lives of its subjects to the extent that the Romans did their citizens; this is in stark contrast to a government, which wants to extract as much control and tax revenue from its subjects as possible. Nabataea would only hire mercenaries if political problems got in the way of business. Its king was perhaps more akin to a CEO, running the financial operations and trade of the civilization, but little else. For this reason, Nabataea is the world's first corporation-as-country, beating the East India Trading Company and the United Fruit Company by two millennia.

Yet the society is still shrouded in mystery, mostly due to the stunning accomplishment of the construction of Petra itself – a city literally hewn from the rock cliffs surrounding it. Regardless of this achievement, the Nabataeans never disregarded their origins as free traders of the desert. Over the span of 400 years, these people of uncertain and nomadic origins rose to a level of power and sophistication that rivaled Rome itself, and then faded from the world stage into obscurity. How did such a proud, powerful civilization suffer such a humble end?

The Nabataeans were a collection of pre-Islamic, Arab nomadic tribes and family groups who coalesced into a vibrant and prosperous urban civilization in one of the most unlikely places in the ancient world: the middle of the Jordanian desert. They took to this new way of life so readily that, by most accounts, their transformation was astonishingly fast; from the vantage point of their neighbors, it was as if the society appeared *ex nihilio* – "out of nothing." Their ability to construct such a city reflects that their society was the combination of two seeming contradictions: The Nabataeans were residents of the harsh Arabic deserts, yet they embraced Hellenic Greek culture, as did many other societies during the time of Alexander's conquests and the immediate aftermath.

They rose from the deserts of northern Arabia during the period of the pre-Alexandrian Persian Empire (539-332 B.C.). The culture gathered around the area of Petra due to its access to trade routes. They still maintained a mostly nomadic existence, but slowly began a lucrative spice trade.

The Nabataeans soon thrived, regardless of their home being practically devoid of rainfall. They overcame this problem and were able to move beyond subsistence living by building vast cisterns and underground wells capable of storing enough fresh water from the region's meager amount of yearly rainfall. The cisterns were capable of sustaining a city of over 20,000 inhabitants through an intricate network of ceramic pipes that relied on gravity and hydraulics to deliver the pressurized water to Petra's citizens.

Their engineering prowess also extended to farming. The Nabataeans developed a method of capturing water which allowed them to plant vineyards and crops on uncultivated, arid land by altering hillsides through contouring. This process caused rainwater to flow downward and gather in valleys. Such methods of planting rows of crops in contours, which ran perpendicular to the slope of the hill rather than parallel, were not adopted widely in the American Midwest until the 1950s. Soil in the rainwater runoff gathered around fruit trees and crops, creating a natural seal that provided water during long dry spells. Through this method, the

Nabataeans transformed the desert into a fertile plain able to sustain a beautiful and unique city at its center. It also prevented soil erosion and preserved the productivity of the farm land.

The challenges of living in the Southern Levant may have contributed to the Nabataeans' creative prowess, but the isolation from neighbors could have been equally beneficial. Inhabiting an area other societies considered to be too remote and forbidding could have given the civilization years or even decades to develop with little worry that a powerful neighbor would swallow them up. All the while, transient populations of merchants who paid tribute in order to trade their goods in Petra influenced the nascent culture and fostered an increasingly wealthy merchant class. These rich individuals wanted to leave their mark on the new civilization and did so by funding monuments, vast tombs, and varied and sophisticated pottery and ceramics that were unique in the Levant.

Architecture, though, is never an inexpensive project, and it had to be funded by considerable revenue sources to design such a building. The Nabataeans were able to raise sufficient revenue by monopolizing trade of the most important luxury item in the ancient world – incense; in particular, through the explosive rise in demand of frankincense in the first millennium B.C. Today, the spice is only recognized as the stuff of Christmas pageants and gifts given by Persian wise men to the infant Jesus. However, frankincense had multiple uses in the ancient world. Israelites used it in the Tabernacle of the First and Second Jerusalem Temples as an ingredient in the perfume of the sanctuary and an accompaniment of the meal-offering. The charred remains of frankincense were also crushed and used to make the distinctive eye-liner seen on ancient Egyptians, as depicted in hieroglyphics of pharaohs. It also had uses in perfumery, traditional medicine, and even skincare.

Due to Nabataea's location between the Mediterranean, Egypt, and Arabia, it oversaw a confluence of trade routes throughout the ancient world, handling not only frankincense, but eventually myrrh, spices, indigo, and other aromatics from Africa, India, China, and beyond. This was the same business that, according to the book of First Kings in the Old Testament, led the Queen of Sheba to visit King Solomon in Jerusalem. The Nabataeans were first intermediaries in the spice trade, ferrying it from Petra to the port cities of Gaza and Alexandria. Yet, as they gained political control of the lands bordering the Arabian frontiers, they took a more active role in both production and distribution.

The Nabataean kings, as befitting their role of being more CEO than emperor in the traditional mold of a Roman ruler, took command in a Hellenistic style more concerned with the well-being of their immediate economy than with expanding their borders through military conquest. When traders passed through Nabataea en route to destinations throughout the Levant and southern Mediterranean, their tributes enriched the kingdom. That wealth fostered a strong merchant class with the kind of dispensable capital that gave rise to patrons of the arts and sponsors of science and architecture. As a result, great monuments and structures were built, including gigantic tombs and statuary, as well as a splendid outdoor amphitheater with a capacity for 6,000 people.

The greatest legacy of the Nabataeans is the city of Petra itself. It was a magnificent fortress carved from the rose-colored sandstone cliffs in the region and a work of art, architecture, and engineering that existed quietly alongside the complex civilizations of Greece, Rome, Persia, and Egypt. Though the city has more ancient origins, having been occupied first by the Edomites before the third century B.C., it was the Nabataeans who transformed it into a monument of architectural and artistic splendor whose beauty and majesty can still be glimpsed among its ruins today.

At the height of their influence, the Nabataeans had established trade routes throughout the Arab world, into the Aegean Islands, and all the way to the Bay of Naples. However, all this building garnered the attention of Rome. As Rome expanded throughout the Levant during the first century A.D., Nabataea became increasingly isolated and pressured to pay tribute to the reigning world power. Rome finally annexed Nabataea in 106 A.D., after which its culture gradually faded into obscurity.

So why did they disappear? This persistent question is the subject of many scholarly theories.

A culture as rich as Nabataea, thriving in a secluded region of northern Arabia, had the potential to wait out any invading force. Indeed, attempted Roman invasions of the area in the first century B.C. had failed, leaving Nabataea one of the few kingdoms free from imperial rule. Rome's vast resources, though, allowed it to enforce persistent influence in the region, and eventually the centers of trade began to shift toward Egypt and other areas.

The Romans had long ago recognized the economic potential of owning Nabataean trade and sought to capitalize on it in areas more conducive to Roman control. Nabataean kings henceforth had to play the game by Roman rules, which required paying tribute to Rome in order to cling to their stake in the incense trade.

By the time Emperor Trajan annexed Nabataea to Rome in 106 A.D., Nabataean culture had begun to fade away. Roman influence brought renewed prosperity to Nabataea, but sadly at the cost of Nabataean independence. The unique aspects of their culture, particularly their pottery, alphabet, and system of government, disappeared.

Some scholars argue that the Nabataeans didn't really disappear but simply assimilated into nearby civilizations or migrated to another trading hub. It is a highly plausible theory, as Nabataean culture was defined less by a unified civilization and more by groups of families and tribes of free Arabs. These people were overseen by a succession of kings who were also considered sheikhs of the tribes. Their common identity was thus quite weak, similar to the idea of being an American prior to the Civil War – it was little more than an academic concept and stood below state identity of being a Virginian or New Yorker. Could these fiercely independent people of the desert simply sacrifice the most vital aspect of their culture – their liberty?

Another theory is that, from rise through fall, the

Nabataean people lived a dual life. They developed a public façade, which, like Petra itself, presented an image of a unified and highly complex society, while on the inside they remained connected to the nomadic desert lifestyle from which they had emerged. This argument also appears to be viable when one takes into account how quickly they rose from the sand to jostle Rome and how equally quickly they were subsumed back into the Roman and Arabic cultures that absorbed them.

The development of their religion offers clues as to the nature of their disappearance; the major Nabataean deities, Al-Uzza and Dushara, were originally depicted as simple blocks of stone hewn out of the surrounding mountainside, known as "god blocks." With Greek and Roman influence, Al-Uzza and Dushara began to take on more anthropomorphic forms, sporting faces and other human features. Byzantine Christianity found easy converts among Petra's population in the fourth-century A.D. A population this quick to pivot from one belief system to another may indeed have had the flexibility to revert to the lifestyle they had enjoyed before their rise as an economic juggernaut.

Others propose that, as the trade that sustained Nabataean power gradually declined, so did their multicultural identity. Vigorous trade fostered interaction with travelers throughout the known world, and it could be postulated that each of these cultures left its mark on Nabataea. This would account for their seemingly vast knowledge of architecture, engineering, and pottery, particularly the fact that all of these aspects of their high culture appeared to reflect influences from Greece, Rome, Egypt, and Aramaea. Their written language was Aramaic, but while some inscriptions seem to indicate that they were Arabs, other evidence indicates that they were Aramaean. This melting pot of influences could indicate that the Nabataeans were highly adaptable, but perhaps unwilling or incapable of sustaining a culture unique to themselves. They were victims of multiculturalism.

Despite unsuccessful attempts by the Romans to muscle in on the spice trade by military force, the trade routes began to shift after Rome's involvement and Petra was left alone in the desert. Overland trade of incense in Southern Arabia declined along with the collapse of the Roman imperial economy. The death knell of Petra came with an earthquake in 363 A.D.

Petra embraced Christianity in this period, but the original society of the Nabataeans appears to have gradually melted back into the desert from whence they arose. They may have returned to their origins to embrace their erstwhile freedom, leaving behind a mystery in the sand and a now-silent rose-colored city of stone.

It is therefore appropriate that Petra's revival in fortune came about due to its association with Indiana Jones and the Last Crusades. Tourists and onlookers will now forever consider the famous temple as holding unfathomable secrets - an apt way to describe the nature of its disappearance.

Chapter 9

The Kingdom of Aksum (100-940 A.D.):
The Trade Empire that Hid a Lost Tribe of Israel and Guarded the Ark of the Covenant

Until recently, a towering granite obelisk stood in Rome's Porta Capena square on the site of the Roman Circus Maximus. It symbolized Italy's Fascist regime and the misguided inauguration of the "new Roman Empire."

But that obelisk was not built by Romans.

The 79-foot tall granite stele, ornately carved with false doors and windows at its top and bottom, only stood in Rome since the time of Mussolini's reign in the 1930s. It had been stolen from a forgotten empire, once the seat of kings who held considerable influence over the economy of the Roman Empire itself. In 2008, the giant monument was returned to its rightful home – the site of a legendary kingdom in Ethiopia where kings traced their lineage back to Solomon.

The ancient civilization of Aksum developed in one of the oldest continuously inhabited regions of the world. References to Ethiopia appear frequently in the works of Homer and Herodotus, considered at that time to be the extent of the known inhabitable world. It is here that civilizations even more ancient than Aksum arose, most prominent among them being the kingdom of D'mt, which was thought to have occupied parts of modern day Eritrea and Ethiopia in the eighth century B.C. Where D'mt had withered by the fourth century B.C., Aksum eventually grew to consolidate the entire region south of Egypt into a mighty economic power.

By the first century A.D., the Aksumite Empire controlled

the entire region south of the Levant. Occupying this key piece of real estate allowed them to wield power and influence that stretched all the way to Rome. The relative remoteness of Aksum prevented it from being an easy mark of conquest, in contrast to civilizations in the Near East and Mesopotamia, which sat at the crossroads of Europe, Asia, and Africa, and were perpetually within the crosshairs of competing states. This security allowed its people the freedom to develop a complex and lively culture.

The level of craftsmanship and production they attained was notable for an antique civilization, putting them on par with the Greeks and other neighboring cultures. Not only were the Aksumites the only ancient African culture to mint coins, they also mined precious metals, produced unique pottery and artifacts, created their own alphabet, and oversaw a complex web of trade routes that interwove China's Silk Road with sea routes to India and land routes into the deep unknown regions of Africa. They were the hub of a commerce network that would eventually collapse and not regain its former status until the Portuguese and Spanish inaugurated the Age of Exploration in the 1500s.

The Aksumite's language and literary accomplishments were centuries ahead of their illiterate neighbors and is still today an important classical language for researchers of the ancient world. Ge'ez, the written language of Ethiopia, was developed in 500 B.C., and the Amharic language of Ethiopia, now spoken by over 20 million people worldwide, has its origins in this ancient script. For the Aksumites, this Semitic language was the language of their ancient church and remains in use in the liturgical celebrations of the Ethiopian Orthodox Church and the Beta Israel community. With their own language and coinage, the Aksumites carved a niche for themselves as the most culturally and industrially advanced empire on the African mainland south of Egypt.

The most important reason that they were able to hold considerable sway over their neighbors was the simple fact that they exported a significant amount of foodstuffs. The Aksumites farmed wheat and barley on a massive scale – a simpler task in the past when the Horn of Africa was more fertile than it is today in its famine-prone form. It was known in the ancient world for its food exports, even though Egypt had a larger reputation as the breadbasket of the Roman Empire. Beyond grains, the Aksumites produced other goods derived from animals and prepared them for export, particularly tortoise shell and ivory. They shipped these exotic goods from their port at Adulis to the distant corners of the ancient world. They were also energetic importers; their traders were known to Romans, Egyptians, and Arabs alike as procurers of precious and exotic items. If one wanted to find a rare or hard-to-find item in the ancient world, he could do far worse than to stroll through the major Aksumite markets.

The culture has only been recognized for its powerful position in the ancient world by historians in recent years. The traditional view of Aksumite culture – perhaps colored by the modern-day difficulties that Ethiopia faces – considered it to be derivative of their neighbors. Scholars regarded the Aksumite culture to be merely an import from Arabia. However, historical artifacts, including the Ge'ez script itself, have determined that the culture was intrinsically African. Thus, not only was Aksum unique at the time, it was one of the world's oldest existing civilizations, with roots of origin reaching back to 2000 B.C., as evidenced by ancient artifacts found in excavations.

Aksum was the first major empire of the ancient world to convert to Christianity, and its Orthodox church traces its origin to a time in which the earliest Christian traditions developed. Their traditional beliefs appear to have been amenable to Christianity; even before converting, the Akumites worshiped a triumvirate of gods that gradually coalesced into a monotheistic belief system. By the fourth century A.D., the Aksumites were a Christian nation, adhering to the liturgical traditions established by the Greek bishop Frumentius, the teacher of Aksum's king Ezana II.

Some Ethiopians, however, claim an even older connection with the God of the Old and New Testaments. Hundreds of thousands of Jews -- racially African but religiously Jewish – forgotten for centuries, were recently found in the northern province in Gondar. The community claimed to have accepted Judaism at the time of the Israeli kings, some three thousand years earlier.

Where do the Ethiopian Jews originally come from? It is impossible to say, but ancient chronicles give us clues. According to a 700-year-old liturgical Ethiopian text, the Aksumite kings trace their lineage back to the marriage between King Solomon and the Queen of Sheba, an African princess who visited the famous Jewish monarch and observed his legendary wisdom firsthand.

Whatever the historical truth of such claims, it is undeniable that the community came under real oppression for their Jewish beliefs. The Ethiopian Jews came under such intense persecution over the centuries by their Muslim and Christian neighbors that the Israeli government started a program to move them to Israel en masse in order to protect them. The resettlement program began such events as Operation Moses, in which 8,000 were airlifted from Sudanese refugee camps during the 1984-1985 famine, and Operation Solomon, where 14,000 more were rescued from Addis Ababa when rebels from Eritrea closed in on the capital. The organized immigration of Ethiopian Jews to Israel formally ended in August 2013 when a plane carrying 450 immigrants arrived in Jerusalem, bringing the three-decade program to an end. In all, 90,000 Ethiopians immigrated to Israel.

For some of the religiously devout, these allegedly ancient bloodlines that connect the Ethiopians to ancient Israel are more than a historical curiosity. To them, it accounts for the identification of Aksum with the Ark of the Covenant. The sacred relic, described in the Book of Exodus as containing the first Torah, Aaron's staff, and the stone tablets on which the Ten Commandments were inscribed, was the center of Jewish worship until the construction of the First Temple by Solomon. It is thought to have been destroyed by the Babylonian destruction of Jerusalem and Solomon's temple in 597 B.C. However, numerous theories have been put forward that it still exists in the Near East or North Africa and is under heavy security. Suggestions as to its final location include Mount Nebo in Israel, South Africa, or – if one is to believe "Raiders of the Lost Ark" – in an unmarked box at a massive warehouse.

The most popular theory, though, is that the Ark's final resting place is in Ethiopia. This theory has been officially endorsed by the Ethiopian Orthodox Church, which has even used the purported ark as a part of ritual processions. The Ark is thought to reside in the chapel within the Church of Our Lady Mary of Zion and has been there since the time of King Menelik I, alleged son of the Queen of Sheba. According to the proponents of this theory, a successive line of monks guards the Ark. After one dies, the next is chosen, each one in turn devoting his life to the protection of the holy relic. The veracity of the holy object is considered to be dubious by most researchers, but these accounts indicate the depth of faith in Ethiopia and the extent to which Christianity played a role in the development of Aksum as an ancient world power.

Yet, the political might of the ancient kingdom had more to do with the changing nature of global trade routes than religion. The strength of Aksum principally related to its location along the coast of the Red Sea and the continual flow of trading vessels in and out of its ports, as well as overland merchants. This trade system was initially catalyzed by the discovery of a direct route to India via the Red Sea, which was a boon to Aksumite development, as it made them the key supplier of Indian imports to Rome. For 400 years, the Aksumites prospered. At the height of its influence, Aksum controlled the eastern seaboard of the Red Sea and caravan routes through Egypt, and stretched from Ethiopia and Eritrea to Yemen and Saudi Arabia across the Red Sea.

An ancient account from a First Century merchant notes Aksum's influence on the ivory trade: "Opposite Mountain Island, on the mainland twenty stadia from shore, lies Adulis, a fair-sized village, from which there is a three-days' journey to Coloe, an inland town and the first market for ivory. From that place to the city of the people called Auxumites there is a five-days' journey more; to that place all the ivory is brought from the country beyond the Nile

71

through the district called Cyeneum, and thence to Adulis."

Arguably, the most notable aspect of Aksumite culture that can still be seen today is the development of its distinctive obelisks. These towering totems were ornately carved granite monuments commemorating its emperors, anchored beneath the ground and reaching skyward to proclaim to the world the glory of Aksum and its kings. The ancient obelisks were symbols of the endurance of a culture that prospered for 1,000 years. It is, therefore, no coincidence that Mussolini decided to install the Great Obelisk in Rome, as he hoped that his fascist state would enjoy similar endurance. Fortunately for the free world, the obelisk did not acquiesce.

By the 9th century A.D., the power and influence of the Aksumites had begun to wane, particularly with the rise and expansion of the Islamic Caliphate to the east. As their new rivals spilled out of Arabia in the mid seventh century, they quickly took control over the Red Sea, pushing the Ethiopian kingdom into isolation. However, the cause of the Aksumite decline cannot be pinned on the caliphate alone. Its decline preceded the appearance of Islam by decades, as it terminated its production of coins in the early seventh century, signaling manufacturing and economic deterioration. Soon afterward, its population receded from the coasts and into the highlands for protection from the invading caliphate. Aksum was abandoned as the capital and Ethiopia lost control over most of its coast and its tributary states by extension. The civilization then disappears from the record.

No single reason adequately explains this decline, and it is the subject of fierce scholarly debate to this day. The most likely explanation points to a number of contributing factors, from environmental changes to political shifts, throughout the region. The rise of Islam most likely had a decisive factor on the Christian Orthodox kingdom. Prior to the growth of the caliphate, the most powerful religion in the region was Christianity, and the Ethiopians enjoyed a certain degree of patronage from other neighboring Christian states, such as the Byzantines to the East and the Coptic kingdoms to the north. By the seventh century, though, Christianity had become a second-class religion in the Horn of Africa and held considerably less power than in earlier times.

Due to the mysterious nature of Aksum's decline, it has taken on a mythical character. Scholars point to a legend in the local history of a queen that rose to power from the south, exterminated the royal bloodline, and destroyed the empire, which had likely already been weakened by successive droughts and the inability of the people to adapt to climate change. Local folklore tells of another Queen Gudit, or "Judith", a follower of Ethiopian Judaism, who burned churches and destroyed ancient texts. These two accounts of a powerful queen have some basis in fact, owing to accounts from contemporary historians of a female usurper who ruled the kingdom at this time. Yet, the myths appear to be later fabrications, as little reliable information about her remains to this day.

Whatever the reason or combination of reasons for its decline, Aksum and its incredible power completely disappeared by the end of the first millennium. It was soon a distant memory to the successor kingdoms that built over their ruins. The stalwart obelisks, many of them toppled by seismic activity, became distant and mysterious anomalies.

Despite the apparent extermination of the ancient Aksumite bloodline and the decline of Aksum as an economic power, a handful of the precise records maintained by the monks of the Ethiopian Orthodox Church have survived since antiquity. A keen interest in Ethiopian culture was revived by African Americans during the latter half of the 20th century, which served to renew interest in Aksum and its cultural influence. Ethiopian dress, cuisine, and traditions were reintroduced to the world in an effort to show that Africa deserved a seat at the table of the world's greatest ancient cultures.

The modern-day interest in the Aksumites has much to do with its last ruling dynasty: the fabled Solomnite kings. They traced their lineage back to the marriage of King Solomon to the Queen of Sheba, proudly claiming Israel's wisest and most powerful king as their forefather. In the tenth century A.D., the ruling Zagwe Dynasty was overthrown by the would-be emperor of Ethiopia, who claimed direct descendancy from the ancient Aksumite royal house. These kings ruled Aksum, and later Ethiopia, with little interruption until 1974.

This dynasty has taken on mythical status among some groups, even causing some to believe that these descendants of King Solomon are messianic figures. The last Ethiopian king, Haile Selassie, is heralded by the Rastafarian religion as the modern messiah due to his role in the Pan Africanism movement of the 1930s. The followers of this African-based spiritual ideology, numbering between 200,000 and 800,000, revere him as the returned messiah of the Bible that will usher in a future gold age of righteousness, prosperity, and eternal peace. Most importantly, he will lead the population of Africa and the African diaspora to freedom. Selassie helped fuel this myth. In 1961, he told a Jamaican delegation to Ethiopia that he would personally give assistance in the matter of repatriation. In 1966, he visited Jamaica and approximately 100,000 Rastafari descended on the Kingston airport. He was unable to exit the plane as the crowd rushed the tarmac.

Today, in Ethiopia and Eritrea, the ancient imperial obelisks still surround the hills above Aksum, the ancient Christian tradition still follows the Orthodoxy using the liturgical language of Ge'ez, and the faithful practice the ancient religion in churches older than the cathedrals of Rome. The Aksumite Kingdom may have fallen into ignominy, but its illustrious spirit lives on.

Chapter 10

The Roanoke Colony (1585-?): The Ghosts of Colonial America

Hamilton McMillan, a North Carolina state legislator in the late 19th Century, enjoyed good relations with his "red bones" neighbors, even though he was mystified by their origins. They had originally received the nickname because of their supposed American Indian lineage; their official name was the Melungeons, which meant "half-breed" in French. The group was thought to be of mixed European, sub-Saharan African, and American Indian ancestry. To make questions of their origin even more confusing, McMillan learned that the tribe considered itself to be the descendants of the doomed Roanoke colony.

At first, this claim seemed far-fetched, as there were no known survivors from the 16th-century settlement. The Melungeons, furthermore, were thought to be descended from mixed-raced unions between free people of color and American Indians. However, McMillan began to notice that many of the "red bones" native words sounded suspiciously like English vernacular used centuries ago. Many of their surnames also matched member lists of the settlement, which disappeared without a trace nearly two centuries before America's independence.

The story of Roanoke is one of America's most enduring unsolved mysteries. Its downfall and disappearance is something of a ghost story told and retold in history classes across the nation. The colonizing of Roanoke Island and its vanishing are fraught with treachery, mismanagement, and ambiguity.

Its story begins with the European race to colonize the New World at the height of the Age of Exploration. In order to compete with the Spanish, who were plundering the Americas for riches in the 1580s, Queen Elizabeth I of England entreated Sir Walter Raleigh to mount an expedition to North America. Its purpose was to put an English presence on the continent, possibly convert American Indians to the Anglican Church before they became Catholic at the hands of Spanish priests, and procure riches of their own.

Raleigh organized a journey west in 1585 that, to many, seemed cursed from the beginning. The voyage was led by Raleigh's cousin, Sir Richard Grenville, and included five ships bound for the island of Roanoke in the province of Virginia, following a scouting journey completed the previous year. It was an all-male colony, designed along the lines of Spanish conquistador groups, and required finding local women. They set out for Roanoke Island's protected shores, which they considered to be a "most pleasant and fertile" land, inhabited by a "loving and faithful" people. Over the course of the next few months, a series of mishaps nearly prevented the expedition from succeeding.

Grenville set out before Raleigh, and his small fleet was battered by storms and accidents. He arrived in Puerto Rico and waited for his cousin to arrive, as they had agreed to reconnoiter there in the event of interference. By the time the first of Raleigh's fleet arrived, Grenville had lost patience and the two ships set out together for America before the other three came. Along the way, Grenville's vessel hit a shoal. All the perishable supplies aboard were lost, but the crew managed to repair the damage and again set sail.

Finally, at the end of June, every member of the fleet arrived and prepared to embark on a life in the New World. The 108 men that were dropped off on Roanoke settled on the northern side of the island and built a defense fort against Spanish intrusion.

The first year of settlement was beset by peril, primarily because of the actions of the colonists. At first, they succeeded in organizing a small village and recognizing local flora and fauna. They built thatched-roof houses and grew maize, potatoes, and grain. Early on, though, an incident with the local Croatoan people, with whom they initially enjoyed pleasant relations by trading beads and trinkets, turned sour. The Croatoans were accused of stealing from the colonists; whether it was true or a fabrication, the charge set the stage for hostilities between the two groups. The colonists struck first, burning a Croatoan village to the ground in retaliation for the perceived theft.

They were then forced to ward off a hostile retaliatory attack by the Croatoans, which they successfully did. It was a tactically prudent but strategically naive decision to make, as the Indians were their best potential trading partners. The colonists were soon in desperate need of food, since they had not yet cultivated their land or built up adequate grain storage.

Grenville returned to England to secure more supplies for the fledgling colony, which had been thrown into internal disagreement and conflict due to the onset of starvation conditions. When he returned to the settlement the following year, he found it abandoned, with the exception of 15 men left to hold down the fort. He imagined the worst, but his fears were quickly put to rest. Grenville learned that the colonists had been visited by his opponent Sir Francis Drake, who had anchored at Roanoke en route back to England with a plunder of treasure. Drake had offered to take the colonists back home with him, to which all had enthusiastically agreed. The English supply ships missed them by only a few days.

Sir Walter Raleigh tried a second time to colonize the island. He established a second charter that addressed the failures of the first colony. First, women and children were added to the group, making it more likely that the men would desire to put down roots. Second, he offered each settler a plot of land in the new city of Raleigh. More signed up for this voyage. The second wave of colonists arrived in July of 1587, settling in the abandoned ruins of the first city. One settler was pregnant when she arrived and soon gave birth to the first English child born in the New World, Virginia Dare, on August 18, 1587.

Yet, the major problems that hampered the original colony had not been resolved. Relations were still poor with the natives, despite Governor John White's attempts to re-establish friendly relations. A reliable food supply was also difficult to secure in the uncultivated land. White went on a supply run to England in order to obtain adequate provisions for the oncoming winter and more troops, as the settlers feared an Indian attack. He dispatched a garrison at the fort and returned to England, but not before leaving instructions to the colonists that if they decide to abandon the settlement or run into trouble, to leave a note.

White promised to return quickly but was prevented from coming back to the colony for three years. It was considerably difficult to cross the Atlantic in the winter, and the captain refused to return to America at that time of year. Furthermore, England was engaged in the Anglo-Spanish War and preparing for an invasion from the mighty Spanish Armada. In 1588, his ship was commandeered in order to hold off Phillip II's navy. White could not return until he hired two small vessels in the spring of 1588. He was further delayed when the greedy captains of these vessels attempted to capture Spanish ships on the outward-bound voyage and pillage them; they themselves were captured and their cargo taken. White couldn't return to the colonies with supplies until 1590, when he travelled with a privateering expedition that agreed to stop at Roanoke on the way back from the Caribbean.

White stepped off the boat, set foot on the island, and arrived to emptiness.

The settlement was completely deserted. None of the 90 men, 17 women, or 11 children he had left were anywhere to be found. White began to explore the empty village to look for clues to this mystery. As he walked through the streets, he noticed that the houses had been methodically dismantled. There was no trace of the colonists, nor any indication of aggression. It was as if they had packed up and left in a quiet and orderly fashion. The only possible clue to be found was the word "Croatoan" written on a post. White concluded that the settlers had moved inland to a more protected area, perhaps among friendlier tribes. Yet, questions still remained. Prior to his departure to England, White had instructed the settlers to carve a Maltese cross on a nearby tree if they had been forced to evacuate the island.

He reasoned that the word "Croatoan" meant that they had moved to Croatoan Island – modern-day Hatteras Island – to seek refuge from natives and possibly obtain easier access to food.

He did not have enough time to learn of the ultimate fate of the settlers. Limited resources and an approaching storm led White's men to refuse to embark on an investigative mission. The next day, his expedition returned to England. It would be 12 more years until Walter Raleigh returned, this time with Samuel Mace. Unfortunately, the explorer was unable to learn of the fates of the settlers due to the lure of profit among the sailors causing the mission to fail. The ship spent considerable time on the Outer Banks to allow the crew to gather highly valuable aromatic woods, such as sassafras, that could be sold for a handsome price back in England.

By the time they set sail for Roanoke, another oncoming storm threatened the voyage. The crew returned to England, and to this day the mystery of the fate of Roanoke remains unsolved.

Investigators are still seeking clues leading to the discovery of the "lost colony" of Roanoke. Multiple theories abound. Several small vessels had been left by White as he returned to England. Some experts suggest that after three years of waiting for supplies from Europe, the colonists decided to try their luck at sea on their own and mounted a return voyage to England. Weather records indicate that the Roanoke settlement was established during the worst three years of drought in a century, and this series of poor growing seasons may indeed have induced the colonists to brave the seas. If that was the case, they must have perished in a storm or died of starvation, since no trace of their ill-fated expedition has been found.

Several accounts of white people living among the local Indians have been noted in historical records, including an accurate map drawn by a colonist in nearby Jamestown in 1607 – 17 years after White's discovery of the abandoned settlement. Inscriptions on the map describe an area where white men were living in the manner of "Iroquois."

According to accounts from the early 1700s, Roanoke's

Croatoan people regularly claimed to have white ancestors. Throughout the 18th and 19th centuries, there are records of sightings of white people among the natives, and Croatoans or Tuscarora people with Caucasian features, such as blond hair or grey eyes.

One of the directives of Captain John Smith, founder of the Colony of Jamestown in 1607, was to investigate the disappearance of the Roanoke colonists. Chief Powhatan of the Weroance is known to have boasted to Smith that members of his tribe had killed all of the Roanoke inhabitants. The chief produced English-made implements that seemed to back up his claim, including iron gear and clothing. However, he may have been bluffing or attempting to impress the foreigner, as forensic evidence to date has yet to turn up a single body. Furthermore, the range of the Weroance is unlikely to have included the Roanoke area.

Smith's investigation was by no means the last. The search for Roanoke's lost colonists continues to be actively pursued. In 2012, evidence was discovered that may indicate that the colonists moved to the mainland. A group of researchers known as the First Colony Foundation examined a map that had been drawn by White at the time of the first expedition. This map had been revised by later settlers who covered one corner of the map with a patch to correct an error. A second patch seemed somewhat arbitrary, and when researchers peeled it back, it revealed what appears to be a fort on the mainland.

The area depicted on the map is privately owned, so investigation is currently prohibited. Even more puzzling is why the patch was placed on the map in the first place, since it does not appear to correct any mistakes. Recalling White's own assessment upon his return to the settlement in 1590, the map clue seems to corroborate his claim that they moved "50 miles into the maine." Unfortunately, White never explored the area to verify his claim, so corroborating evidence has yet to be provided.

Of all the possible explanations, perhaps the most persistent is the assimilation theory. Accounts by members of the Lumbee tribe, native to North Carolina, have claimed since the early 18th century that they shared surnames with the original colonists and knew how to read, write, and speak English. These claims have been attested by local inhabitants for over a century, and even prompted legislator Hamilton McMillan to help pass the "Croatoan Bill," officially identifying the local Native Americans as Croatoans.

Another intriguing aspect to the Lumbee is their nebulous origin. They are known to be native to the region, but have a lineage that is difficult to discern, and many do in fact have Anglicized surnames and European features. This may indicate that they are indeed an offshoot of the Croatoan tribe. However, this claim is not as unique as it sounds, considering that knowledge of English among American Indians is attested by the presence of European explorers since the early 1600s. Natives eager for trading opportunities quickly learned a smattering of the language, the most famous example being Squanto, who acted as a mediator between the Pilgrims of Plymouth Rock in modern-day Massachusetts and the New England tribes, following their arrival in 1620.

Until the mainland property can be investigated, the mainland exodus of Roanoke's colonists cannot be verified. Until a forensic investigation produces any bodies, no theory of the settlement's disappearance carries more weight than another.

The mystery endures and the case has not been closed, making the Roanoke colony the longest open investigation in the history of America.

Conclusion

Looking to the Past to Understand the Future

Lost civilizations still have an inordinate influence on modern society. It's a strange statement to make, as a lost civilization, by its very definition, disappeared and its survivors did not live to tell the tale. Yet, a quick survey of pop culture finds that the idea of lost civilizations and social collapse are currently resounding with a very wide audience.

One needs to look no further than the popularity of apocalypse-themed and dystopian movies. The box office in 2013 saw *World War Z*, the blockbuster based on the best-selling book, starring Brad Pitt watching as the world is quickly subsumed by the flesh-hungry undead. The underlying tension in the film is how quickly and unstoppably the virus spreads through the earth; civilizations are wiped out in a matter of days, and the strongest defenses in our arsenal are rendered useless. Another highly anticipated dystopian drama included *The Hunger Games: Catching Fire*, in which the protagonist, Katniss Everdeen, struggles to survive a battle-to-the-death competition run by a wealthy oligarchy that ruthlessly exploits its poverty-stricken outlying provinces.

Comedies that came out the same year did *World War Z* one better. *This is the End* features Seth Rogen and his group of stoner friends doing their best to ride out a literal interpretation of the Biblical Rapture. Another comedy, *The World's End*, sees Simon Pegg and Nick Frost do battle with robots that control the world's information network. The pub-crawlers convince the robot masters to leave Earth through a drunken tirade, resulting in the destruction of Earth's technology and mass media.

The fascination with the apocalypse at the box office – and, to a lesser extent, television series such as *The Walking Dead* and books such as *The Last Detective*, in which a sleuth solves crimes under the shadow of a deadly asteroid only months away from colliding with earth – seem to have resonated well with modern audiences. They not only rake in money at the box office or from advertisers, but they seem to have struck a deep psychological chord and resonated subconsciously with the public.

What is the source of this existential crisis that has audiences seeking out apocalypse-themed entertainment? It is an interesting sociological question, one that Alissa Wilkinson tackled from a religious standpoint in an essay in Christianity Today. She theorizes that in the early 21st century, the death of millions is a very real possibility – whether through a terrorist attack, nuclear war, ecological disaster, or viral outbreak.

Perhaps experiencing the end of the world over and over again in the form of entertainment makes it less terrifying, she writes. We transform it from a shapeless fear to a manageable threat, like disaster preparedness in the face of an earthquake. We can even develop ironic detachment from the event, making it powerless in our minds. We have what postmodern critic Jean Baudrillard said is characteristic of our ironic, self-aware culture: a "cool smile" of knowingness in the face of fear and manifold terrors. Thus, our ability to make jokes about it tames the event and renders it powerless.

In the same way, entertainers have treated the disappearance of entire civilizations with an air of humor. While movie producers may tackle the issue of Atlantis for different reasons than a zombie apocalypse, they very well could be addressing the same underlying issues. Perhaps treating lost civilizations with humor is a means to trivialize the way they disappeared and mitigate the existential fear that it could happen to us again.

In the 2012 edition of Simpsons' annual Treehouse of Horror episode, the Maya Empire receives such a humorous treatment. The episode opens with Homer being prepped as a human sacrifice to appease the gods and prevent the apocalypse. Not wanting to lose his head in the matter (pun intended), he manages to have Moe's Maya doppelganger beheaded in his place. It doesn't work. The sacrifice goes wrong, angering the Maya deities, who promise to tear the earth apart in 2012 in an act of vengeance. Flash forward to the present, where larger-than-life Maya gods raze Springfield, and the rest of the planet, to the ground. Never has the apocalypse been depicted in such gruesome detail, and through the eyes of such yellow-hued characters with four fingers.

Aside from the use of humor as a defense mechanism, another reason that the idea of a civilization disappearing is so alien is that it has not happened in the modern era. There are cases of entire cities being abandoned, as in the case of ghost towns that dot the American West, war-torn cities in Libya, or, most famously, Chernobyl in Ukraine. Still, none of these examples approach the scale of an entire nation-state disappearing, being abandoned, or even being utterly wiped out as was the case of the civilizations under consideration in this book. It's not as if the Democratic Republic of Congo had a thriving civilization until 2005 and then completely disappeared. Yes, it is a war-torn region with serious economic, social, cultural, and military tensions that have led to mass slaughter and disaster, but nothing approaching the scale of its entire society vanishing.

The assumption with such societies that were completely abandoned is that a terrible disaster occurred. Although, as we have seen repeatedly in this book, the far more likely scenario is that they fell into gradual decline until their final inhabitants finally left or were assimilated into nearby cultures. The Maya civilization peaked at approximately 900 A.D., but fell into irreversible decline by 1500 when the Spaniards arrived. However, it had not disappeared by this point and still limped along. No cataclysmic event fell upon it; the result was most likely due to the agricultural base not being able to support the population and political instability tearing apart the civilization. It was most likely absorbed into neighboring states, making the entire area weak and ripe for Spanish conquest.

To get a better idea of how civilizations really disappear, it is useful for us to consider a widely misunderstood event in history. Let us look at the story of the decline of the Great Library of Alexandria.

The royal library in Alexandria, Egypt, was one of the largest and most significant libraries of the ancient world. Its directors attempted to house all the books of the time, including works by the greatest thinkers and writers of antiquity, such as Homer, Plato, Socrates, and many more. It was built during the reign of Ptolemy I Soter in the third century B.C., and is believed to have been destroyed in a huge fire 2,000 years ago. Many works of science, mathematics, and literature were permanently lost.

Today, the idea of a 'Universal Library' has attained mythical status. There is a belief that, due to this tragic loss, human knowledge suffered an irreparable setback for centuries. This idea is found in Carl Sagan's "Cosmos." The famous scientist lamented that we cannot fully grasp what wonderful treasures were permanently destroyed: "We do know that of the 123 plays of Sophocles in the Library, only seven survived. One of those seven is *Oedipus Rex*. Similar numbers apply to the works of Aeschylus and Euripides. It is a little as if the only surviving works of a man named William Shakespeare were *Coriolanus* and *A Winter's Tale*, but we had heard that he had written certain other plays, unknown to us but apparently prized in his time, works entitled *Hamlet, Macbeth, Julius Caesar, King Lear, Romeo and Juliet*."

Sagan goes on to say that were it not for the Great Library's destruction, the Dark Ages would have never happened, and modern science would be centuries ahead of where we are today. The reader is left to image that, in this hypothetical world of advanced technology, we would have cures for all known diseases, live 200 years, and ride hover boards such as those in Back to the Future 2. So what happened?

The Great Library was conceived and opened in Alexandria, one of the greatest centers of learning and culture in the ancient world. During the reign of Ptolemy II, the idea of the Universal Library seemed to have taken shape. More than 100 scholars were housed within the museum, whose job was to carry out scientific research, lecture, publish, translate, copy, and collect not only original manuscripts of Greek authors (allegedly including the private collection of Aristotle himself), but also translations of works from Egypt, Assyria, Persia, and the rest of the world.

One story says that the hunger of Ptolemy III for knowledge was so great that he decreed that all ships docking at the port should surrender their manuscripts to the authorities. Copies were then made by official scribes and delivered to the owners, while the original manuscripts were filed away. An estimated half million documents were in the library.

So who destroyed such an esteemed resource, and why would they do that? Ancient sources differ greatly on who is responsible for the destruction and when it occurred. There is, however, an idea as widespread as it is incorrect that there was one major destruction by one group of people; the culprits blamed are Byzantine Christians in 391 A.D. and the Rashidun Caliphate in 640 A.D. One story holds that when the Islamic caliphate conquered Alexandria and heard about a magnificent library containing all the knowledge of the world, many soldiers were anxious to see it, but the Caliph refused to allow the continued existence of pagan books. He stated, "[these books in the library] will either contradict the Qur'an, in which case they are heresy, or they will agree with it, so they are superfluous." The manuscripts were then gathered together and used as fuel for the 4,000 bathhouses in the city. Legend has it that the massive number of scrolls kept the bathhouses of Alexandria heated for six months. This account is almost definitely false, as it was written down 300 years after the supposed event by the thirteenth century Christian scholar Gregory Bar Hebraeus. Even if this account is correct, the library in question was almost certainly not *the* library at Alexandria.

The truth of the matter is that the so-called greatest catastrophe of the ancient world never took place on the scale often supposed. The library wasn't destroyed in one fell swoop by an invading army, but by centuries of neglect by a society no longer interested in classical learning. The citizens of Alexandria themselves let the pillars of the library crumble long before foreign armies set fire to its remains. This is the lesson of the Great Library: knowledge often isn't destroyed by one act of a tyrant, but by a society at large neglecting its own past.

The lesson also pertains to the death of civilizations. Why do they ultimately fall? We don't want to believe it, but the guilty party is almost always us. This was the conclusion reached by historian William Durant, who spent 40 years writing his magnum opus "The Story of Civilization". In it, he considered 2,500 years of human society and the moral frameworks that allowed them to survive, thrive, or decline. The upshot of his extensive research was that, for any civilization to die, the mortal wound that signaled its imminent demise was nearly always self-inflicted:

"A great civilization is not conquered from without until it has destroyed itself from within."

Also by Michael Rank

History's Most Insane Rulers: Lunatics, Eccentrics, and Megalomaniacs from Emperor Caligula to Kim Jong Il

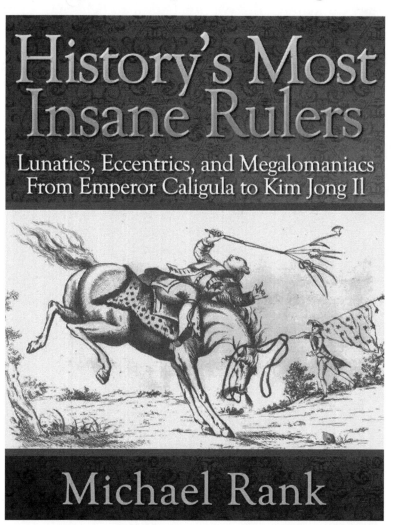

Turn the page to read an excerpt

Chapter 1:

Roman Emperor Caligula (12-41 A.D.)

How to Rule an Empire by Appointing Your Horse Senator

When Salvador Dali set out to paint a depiction of the infamous Roman Emperor Caligula in 1971, he chose to depict the thing nearest and dearest to the crazed emperor's heart: his horse Incitatus. The painting *"Le Cheval de Caligula"* shows the pampered pony in all his royal glory. It is wearing an opulent crown and clothed in fine garments. While the gaudy clothing of the horse is historically correct, for once in his life the Spanish surrealist artist is guilty of severe understatement.

Emperor Caligula, who reigned from 37-41 A.D., was the first emperor with no memory of the pre-Augustan era and therefore had no compunction about establishing a personality cult, ruling with absolute autocracy, demanding his subjects' worship, and treating his horse better than royalty. According to the Roman historian Suetonius, he gave Incitatus 18 servants, a marble stable, an ivory manger, rich red robes, and a jeweled collar. He required that those passing by bow to his horse and demanded that it be fed oats mixed with flex of gold and wine delivered by fine goblets. Dignitaries were forced to tolerate the horse as a guest of honor at banquets. This episode was but one example of the deranged excesses to which Caligula lived and what led to his violent death at the hands of his enemies.

In the four short years that Gaius Julius Caesar Augustus Germanicus (Caligula) served as emperor of Rome, he built for himself a reputation as a man who was committed wholly to his lusts at the expense of his empire. He used his authority, influence and wealth to satisfy his sexual appetite, build his own ego and antagonize the Roman senate. Such behavior is thought to have been the primary reason he also went down in history as the first Roman emperor to be assassinated.

As the third child born to Germanicus (the legendary Roman general and adopted son of the emperor Tiberius) and grandson of the emperor Augustus on his mother's side, Gaius had grown up around Roman soldiers and powerful leaders. His youth was rife with difficulties. In 19 A.D., Caligula's father died under questionable circumstances, leaving his mother, Agrippina the Elder, to manage a strenuous relationship with the emperor Tiberius. Shortly after the death of his father, Caligula was sent to live with his great-grandmother, Livia. When she died two years later, he was sent to his grandmother, Antonia.

When the emperor Tiberius took ill and secluded himself on the island of Capri, he called for Caligula to be with him there on the island. In 31 A.D., Caligula accepted the invitation and went to tend to his adoptive grandfather. During that time, emperor Tiberius ordered the exile of Caligula's mother and two brothers. They later died, leaving Caligula as the sole male heir of Germanicus.

It is said that even in his illness, Tiberius could tell that Caligula, whom he had appointed joint successor along with his grandson, Tiberius Gemmellus, was not suitable to reign. The emperor referred to him as a viper that he thought would be unleashed on all of Rome. So Caligula was assigned only menial tasks and held no major offices between 31 and 37 A.D. When Tiberius died in 37 A.D., the Roman people received their new emperor with open arms, largely based on the fact that his father, Germanicus, had been so popular and well-loved. They were hopeful for a ruler who would demonstrate more warmth and charity than had Tiberius, who was notably isolated and stingy during his decades-long reign.

The beginning of Caligula's rule went well. He was a strong leader -- compassionate, smart and decisive. His first order of business was to pay off all of the former emperor's debts. He also honored his slain family by retrieving their remains and giving them a proper Roman burial. He gave the

Praetorian guard a handsome bonus, recalled all exiles, and compensated those whom he thought had been wrongly taxed.

Not long into his reign, however, he fell ill and is said to have slipped into a coma. When he awoke, he was a very different man. Caligula had Tiberius Gemmellus killed and began to pursue the sexual appetite he had for his female siblings. He particularly liked his sister, Drusilla, whom he later married and impregnated. Not only did he have conjugal relations with them but he also prostituted them out to other men, effectively turning the palace into a brothel. After Drusilla's death, Caligula married twice more. Both marriages were short-lived. In 38 A.D., just one year after taking office, he married a fourth time to Milonia Caeconia.

Caligula was not at all concerned about the expansion of his empire, nor did he allocate any resources to defeating enemies. In just a few months, he managed to waste the entire fortune left by the emperor Tiberius, a fortune it had taken the former emperor 22 years to collect in tribute. In an effort to increase the amount of money available for his personal use, Caligula ordered all wealthy citizens to name him as the sole heir to their estates upon their deaths. Once that law was in place, he then began a campaign of falsely accusing, fining and killing wealthy citizens to get their money. He also tried and killed his wealthiest subjects for treason on charges of blasphemy so that he might receive their estates. He levied taxes on everything from marriage to prostitution and caused starvation in parts of his empire by claiming large areas of arable land for his own private use. He auctioned the lives of gladiators and claimed the plunder that soldiers had acquired from spoils during war.

Despite the fact that he quickly depleted the treasury and began heavily taxing his subjects, Caligula embarked on several vanity construction projects. He wanted a giant floating bridge built across the Bay of Baiae (Naples) in order to prove wrong the astrologer Trasyllus, who said that "Caligula had no more chance of becoming emperor than of crossing the bay of Baiae on horseback." According to the

Roman historian Suetonius he crafted a solution by doing the following:

"He devised a novel and unheard of kind of pageant; for he bridged the gap between Baiae and the mole at Puteoli, a distance of about thirty-six hundred paces, by bringing together merchant ships from all sides and anchoring them in a double line, after which a mound of earth was heaped upon them and fashioned in the manner of the Appian Way. Over this bridge he rode back and forth for two successive days attended by the entire Praetorian guard and a company of his friends in Gallic chariots."

As he rode back and forth on horseback, Caligula made sure to wear the breastplate of Alexander the Great to shore up his military bona fides. He never actually attempted to go to war, but he did commission the construction of two large war ships that eventually burned without ever having been sailed. The closest he came was in 39-40 A.D. when he went to Gaul and marched to the shores with the military with the intent of invading Britain. Before his army launched its attack, he ordered them to stop and collect seashells. He called these the "spoils of the conquered ocean" and ordered his troops home.

Caligula was perpetually disrespectful of the Senate, who, during the reign of Tiberius had done much of the decision-making on their own, as Tiberius was quite anti-social. In response to their disapproval of him, Caligula did what he could to shame, embarrass and humiliate senate members, both individually and collectively. One famous incident involved his beloved horse, Incatitus, whom Caligula clothed in the finest robes, suitable for most any member of the nobility. Often times when invitations were sent from the palace, they were in the horse's name, and Incatitus was allowed to eat dinner at the emperor's table . It was also said by some Roman historians that Caligula attempted to make Incatitus either a senator or a priest before the emperor's death.

Caligula fully embraced emperor worship and encouraged others to worship him as a god. While previous emperors tolerated this practice, he allowed it and attempted to require it in the Roman provinces. Caligula tried to construct a huge statue of himself inside the Temple in Jerusalem, the center of Jewish worship. This action would have nearly guaranteed a revolt from the Jews, who would have considered the construction a pagan slap to the face of their religion. Herod Agrippa, the descendant of the man who slaughtered dozens of infants in an attempt to kill Jesus, even considered this a terrible idea and convinced the emperor to relent.

It was this consistent and unrelenting disrespect that eventually led to his murder. In early 41 A.D., in a secluded hall in the basement of the palace, Caligula was stabbed 30 times in an attack led by Cassius Chaerea, a guard whom Caligula had humiliated on multiple occasions. The painful and bloody attack didn't kill the emperor right away. But by the time his guards found him, the conspirators were long gone, and he eventually succumbed to his injuries. His wife Caeconia and their infant child were murdered as well.

Few sources contemporary with his life have survived, and his legacy is a bit open to embellishment. Nevertheless, nearly all historians agree that his cruel temperament and extravagance defined him as an emperor. They made for a legacy that far surpassed any positive contributions he gave to Rome.

End of this excerpt.

Enjoyed the preview?

BUY NOW ON AMAZON

Connect With Michael

I hope you have enjoyed this book and learned much about history's greatest lost civilizations.

You can connect with me on my homepage at http://michaelrank.net. Here you can find podcasts, blog posts, and other bits about history. You can also download a free book on Norse and Germanic mythology.

About the Author

Michael Rank is a doctoral candidate in Middle East history. He has studied Turkish, Arabic, Persian, Armenian, and French but can still pull out a backwater Midwestern accent if need be. He also worked as a journalist in Istanbul for nearly a decade and reported on religion and human rights.

He is the author of the #1 Amazon best-seller "From Muhammed to Burj Khalifa: A Crash Course in 2,000 Years of Middle East History," and "History's Most Insane Rulers: Lunatics, Eccentrics, and Megalomaniacs From Emperor Caligula to Kim Jong Il."

One Last Thing

If you enjoyed this book, I would be grateful if you leave a review on Amazon. Your feedback allows me to improve current and future projects.

To leave a review all you need to do is search for this book on Amazon, and you will be taken directly to its sales page. Make it as short or as long as you prefer.

Thank you again for your support!

16477359R00063

Made in the USA
San Bernardino, CA
04 November 2014